YOUR TOWNS & CITIES IN WOR

ABERDEEN

AT WAR 1939–45

For my Parents

YOUR TOWNS & CITIES IN WORLD WAR TWO

ABERDEEN
AT WAR 1939–45

CRAIG ARMSTRONG

Pen & Sword
MILITARY
AN IMPRINT OF PEN & SWORD BOOKS LTD.
YORKSHIRE – PHILADELPHIA

First published in Great Britain in 2020 and reprinted in 2021 by
Pen & Sword Military
An imprint of
Pen & Sword Books Ltd
Yorkshire – Philadelphia

ISBN 978 1 47389 916 2

Printed and bound in the UK on FSC accredited paper by 4edge Ltd, Essex, SS5 4AD
Typeset by Aura Technology and Software Services, India.

Pen & Sword Books Limited incorporates the imprints of Atlas, Archaeology,
Aviation, Discovery, Family History, Fiction, History, Maritime, Military, Military
Classics, Politics, Select, Transport, True Crime, Air World, Frontline Publishing,
Leo Cooper, Remember When, Seaforth Publishing, The Praetorian Press,
Wharncliffe Local History, Wharncliffe Transport, Wharncliffe True Crime and
White Owl.

For a complete list of Pen & Sword titles please contact

PEN & SWORD BOOKS LIMITED
47 Church Street, Barnsley, South Yorkshire, S70 2AS, England
E-mail: enquiries@pen-and-sword.co.uk
Website: www.pen-and-sword.co.uk

Or
PEN AND SWORD BOOKS
1950 Lawrence Rd, Havertown, PA 19083, USA
E-mail: Uspen-and-sword@casematepublishers.com
Website: www.penandswordbooks.com

Contents

CHAPTER 1

1939 – A Storm Breaks

With the formal announcement of war, the people of Aberdeen began to take blackout restrictions far more seriously and the warden service and the police began to enforce them in a draconian fashion. Heavy blackout curtains and coverings became the norm for everyone while shopkeepers had to also screen lights with dark material and cover skylights. The blackout would become a regular and widely accepted, though often grumbled about, fact of wartime life for several years.

An Aberdeen Housewife fitting her Blackout. (People's Journal)

An Aberdeen Shopkeeper fits a Blackout Device to a Shop Light. (People's Journal)

For others, the initial impact of war had limited effects as they went about many of their normal working routines. However, there would be no 'business as usual' campaign as had been the norm for the first years of the First World War. For coastal Aberdeenshire communities and those alongside the rivers of the county, fishing was an important way of making a living. For those who worked aboard the trawler fishing fleets, however, the work would not remain normal for long. Many had already been called up for service with the RNR (Royal Naval Reserve) while for those who remained behind fishing would become even more dangerous due to enemy action.

One of the most visible ways in which the war could be seen was that people were ordered never to leave the house without their gasmask. With many people expecting an immediate attack, it would seem that most Aberdonians conscientiously obeyed the

Veteran Fisherman George Christie of Wood Street, Torry, Organises his Lines as a Trawler Steams into Harbour. (People's Journal)

Above left: *A Dee Eel Fisherman empties his catch into a Storage Cage.* (People's Journal)

Above right: *A Dee Eel Fisherman about to sink his Storage Cage.* (People's Journal)

Civilians carrying gasmasks in Aberdeen. (Aberdeen Weekly Journal)

instructions and the necessity of carrying the respirators was continually reinforced by the local press.

The news of the sinking of the trans-Atlantic passenger liner the SS *Athenia* by the German submarine *U-30* on the first day of the war was met with a mix of anger and shock. Decried as a war crime by the British government, the disaster left several Aberdeen families facing an anxious wait for news of loved ones who had been on board. In addition to family and friends of the passengers there were also several crew members who were Aberdonians or had family in Aberdeen. These included the master of the *Athenia*, Captain James Cook. A Greenock man, Captain Cook's sister, Mrs C. Nicholson, lived at 67 Louisville Avenue, Aberdeen (her husband had recently retired from his position as manager of Boots at 133 Union Street).

It was known that more than twenty passengers from Aberdeen were aboard the *Athenia*, mainly natives of the city who were returning to their homes in Canada or the USA. Of these there was only one man and there were several mothers with small children. One girl, 9-year-old Ruby Mitchell was travelling back to her home in Canada alone following a visit to her grandmother in Aberdeen. Amongst the families were Aberdonians Mr and Mrs Insch who were returning to their home in the USA with their 13-year old daughter, Bunty.

Two days later, telegrams began to reach Aberdeen bringing news of the fate of those on board. By the end of day on 5 September it had been established that at least twelve of the Aberdeen passengers had been rescued. The first news to come through was that of Mr and Mrs Insch. Shortly afterwards, Messrs MacKay Brothers indicated that they had received word that six of the passengers who had booked passage with them were safe. This was followed by news that three other Aberdonian passengers were safe. Miss Dora Smith of 188 Great Western Road arrived back home on 5 September. Telling her story to reporters, Miss Smith said that she had sailed with her cousin, Mrs Frances McKenzie and her young daughter, Abigail, and had been sitting with them when the torpedo struck. She said that they knew immediately what had happened and made for the top deck but became separated in the confusion. Miss Smith then found herself in a lifeboat which was being lowered when she said she heard another torpedo hit (in all likelihood this was probably an internal explosion). Miss Smith reported that most people remained calm and that the ship's officers set a wonderful example, but that some girls did panic and jumped into the sea. While in the lifeboats she witnessed a surfaced submarine fire a shot, which missed, at the stricken liner. Miss Smith spent ten hours in the lifeboat, which, according to her 'seemed like ten years' before they were picked up and subsequently landed at Glasgow. She made her way home to Aberdeen and was met at Aberdeen Joint Station by her father and brother, who helped her along the platform following her ordeal.

By the end of the day it was clear that known survivors included: Mr and Mrs Insch and their daughter, Mrs Margaret Hannah, Mrs Margaret Jamieson and her son William, Miss Dora Smith, Miss H.M. Taylor, Miss Minnie Davidson, Mrs Rogers, Miss Gladys Stronach and Mrs M. Buckerfield.

Over the course of the week news continued to trickle through of those who had been on board the *Athenia*. Mrs Balneaves, who had secured the last berth on the liner, was confirmed as being safe despite having suffered a broken leg when her lifeboat fell into the sea. Mrs F. Dexter cabled her sister in Aberdeen to say that she and her husband were safe although they had been separated during the disaster. It was also reported that 5-year-old Jacqueline Hayward had been saved and was now in Falkirk with her family. Miss Hayward had been accompanied by her mother and 9-year-old sister, Margaret. She had been sitting on her mother's knee and could only remember a loud boom before finding herself in the sea and seeing her doll floating away. Her mother and sister were saved and taken aboard the SS *City of Flint* bound for Nova Scotia. The children's grandmother, Mrs Wright of 18 Primrosehill Drive,

Mrs Buckerfield
(Aberdeen Weekly.
Journal)

was very relieved to hear that they were safe, but was devastated days later when her daughter's husband cabled her to inform her that little Margaret had died of a brain injury on the *City of Flint*. Others to be named on a new list of survivors included Miss Annie McComb, Mr and Mrs McLean and their son Jack, Mrs Alice Pocklington, Mrs Forbes and 9-year-old Ruby Mitchell.

Just two days after the declaration of war there was a tragic accident in Aberdeen. A lorry with a large load of timber, belonging to Messrs Carrie & Sons of Lawton, Dundee, collided with a tramcar at the junction of Anderson Drive and Great Northern Road in Woodside. The lorry was travelling north and collided with the city-bound tram as it emerged from Anderson Drive. The crash left one dead and fifteen injured. So great was the impact of the collision that the two vehicles became locked together and a gang of men from the Transport Department had to work for three hours to prise them apart. The damage was obvious, the tram had a huge hole in the front and lower deck seating had been torn from the frames and the lorry cab had been completely shattered. Tram driver, Mr David E. Brown (38) of 6 Jasmine Place, was terribly injured in the collision and died several hours later in the Royal Infirmary. The lorry driver, Mr Syme, and his mate, Mr Duncan, were extremely fortunate in that the damage just missed them and they were able to pull themselves out of the wreckage. Mr Syme suffered a slight knee injury and Mr Dunlop minor injuries to his chin, hand and leg.

Others injured were tram conductor William W. Clark (25) of 23 Perrier Gardens, William Coull Christie (40) of 2 Manor Walk, Miss Agnes Young (16) of 52 Manor Avenue, Miss Violet Gibb (18) of 29 Logie Avenue, Miss Jean Flora Watt (24) of 8 Manor Drive, Miss Beryl Low (17) of 32 Logie Avenue and Miss Amelia Sim Calder Mitchell (19) of 32 Manor Avenue.

Above: Jacqueline Hayward. (Aberdeen Weekly Journal)

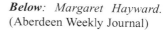

Below: Margaret Hayward. (Aberdeen Weekly Journal)

The screams of passengers as they were thrown violently forward amidst splintered wreckage and shards of glass drew bystanders to their aid; many had very fortunate escapes. Mr A. Leslie of 59 Logie Place was on the rear upper deck of the tram and was thrown into the air by the force of the collision. He struck the tram roof and was hurled forward landing at the front of the upper deck. Mr Leslie walked away from the crash but subsequently had to be taken to hospital. He had only just resumed work after a period of unemployment. Another of the upper deck passengers, Miss Annie Brodie (19) of 5 Manor Walk, ran home following the crash despite the splinters of glass in her face and head. Miss Brodie had lost her shoes in the crash, along with her respirator. Mrs Cruickshank of 30 Logie Avenue was seated at the front of the tram but did not actually see the crash. She explained how she was sitting with her fare ready when all of a sudden there was 'a terrible noise of breaking glass and splinters flew about in all directions'.[1] She suffered a dislocated shoulder, knee and head injuries. Two lower deck passengers, Miss Evelyn Geddes and Mr Robert Styles, both of whom lived at 3 Manor Walk, were knocked unconscious in the crash while 14-year-old Irene Robb of 16 Manor Drive was physically unhurt but suffering from shock.

In addition to those who were injured on the initial crash, a cyclist, William John Hadden (16) of 4 Logie Place, received a minor leg injury when his cycle collided with an ambulance which was on its way to the scene of the accident.

There was another road accident in Aberdeen on that day, this one fatal. Ten-year old William Cooper of 13 Seaton Drive, Aberdeen, was struck by a lorry as he ran across King Street near Bridge of Don. The wheel of the lorry went over William's leg and he suffered a compound fracture and severe shock. Despite being rushed to the Sick Children's Hospital, William died shortly after 6pm.

The locked together wreckage of tram and lorry. (Aberdeen Weekly Journal)

Of the many evacuees who were sent to Aberdeenshire, those who were sent to the Balmoral Estate on Royal Deeside probably had the strangest experience. By 6 September over seventy had arrived from working class areas of Glasgow and found that their new surroundings could not have been more different from the crowded environment that they had left behind. A score of the evacuees were housed in Balmoral Castle itself while more than fifty were welcomed at Abergeldie. Many more were taken in by employees on the Balmoral Estate.

Just days after their arrival they had been welcomed into their new schools. For many this was time spent in local schools but under the charge of their own, familiar, teachers but for some staying at Balmoral it meant attending the newly-formed school which took place in the ballroom adjoining the castle. The fine weather in mid-September meant that many classes at Balmoral were taken outside next to the river in picturesque, if unfamiliar, surroundings. Although many of the children would doubtless have been nonplussed and bewildered by their new environment, others rapidly adjusted to the new sights and experiences offered by rural life in north-east Scotland. The teachers from the south were unanimous in their opinion that the people of the north-east had welcomed them very warmly and had done everything in their power to help the children (and teachers) adjust to their new surroundings. One of the many new experiences for many of these evacuees was that many of them faced a long walk from their new, temporary, home to school. One Glaswegian headmaster remarked that although some of his pupils had to walk three or four miles to school 'not one of them has shirked the walk. They tell me they enjoy it.'[2]

Glaswegian children from St Annes School Crownpoint Road enjoy an outdoor lesson on the Balmoral Estate.

Many Aberdeenshire fishermen were members of the Royal Naval Reserve (RNR) and had been called up to serve on minesweeping trawlers and other small but vitally important vessels. One of the first servicemen from the area to lose his life was such a man. On 11 September Petty Officer John Hudson Charters Dickson Ballard (36), known to friends as Jack, was walking along the bank of the River Yare at Great Yarmouth with a friend when he fell into the river. An attempt to save him by a police constable failed and a search of several hundred yards of riverbank failed to reveal any sign of him. The tragedy was made all the worse by the fact that his father had drowned just a few hundred yards away while at Great Yarmouth with the pre-war herring fleet. Petty Officer Ballard was a married man and left a widow, Margaret, and their three children at their home at 9 Sinclair Road, Torry, and, at the time of his death, was assigned to the minesweeping trawler HMS *Ebor Wyke*.[3] His body was later recovered and his funeral took place at Trinity Cemetery, Aberdeen, on 22 September. Friends, many in service uniforms, were present and the service was conducted by Skipper Crockett of the Royal National Mission to Deep Sea Fishermen and Mr James W. Morrice of the British Sailors' Society. The pallbearers were Ballard's son, David, his brothers David and Albert, his uncle Albert and William Smith and R. McIntosh.

With the importance of manning the fishing fleet of Aberdeen and the probable increase in profitability in the wartime market, there was a willingness on the part of trawler owners to present their employees with better wages. In mid-September it was agreed that an extra 1s per day would be brought in immediately for enginemen and deckhands alongside a 2d on the net poundage of the vessels. This meant that a chief engineer would now receive 15s per day, a second engineer 13s 6d per day, deck hand trimmers 11s 6d and deck hands and cooks 10s 6d. It was also agreed that if the national agreement, which was to be decided in London, was of a higher rate it would apply to Aberdeen trawlermen. The agreement also provided war risk insurance and the payment of a stipulated rate of compensation to men who were injured in the course of fishing operations during the war.

While many in Aberdeen adjusted to wartime conditions and worried over what the future might bring, some in the church were embarking on a moral crusade to restrict the availability of alcohol. At a Presbytery meeting held on 12 September the subject of the limiting of public house licensing hours was introduced by the Rev. D.G. Baine, of Torry, on behalf of the Temperance Committee. The committee 'earnestly' requested that magistrates should order all public houses to close earlier than the government-recommended 9.30pm and that conditions under which special licences were issued should be reconsidered and substantially reduced.

The first attempts at British propaganda were rather clumsy. Strict rules over censorship combined with worries over revealing losses in case it eroded morale and a lack of trust in the steadiness of the average member of the British public, meant that the Aberdeen public, along with everyone else, were often informed of early victories and triumphs despite the realities of the wartime situation. In mid-September, clearly anxious to show that Britain was on the front foot, the newspapers in Aberdeenshire carried overblown and hyperbolic accounts of the first raid on German territory. The raid (which became known as the Kiel Raid despite the targets actually being naval units in the harbours of Wilhelmshaven and Brunsbüttel) had actually taken place on the day following the announcement of war but news was not widely released until ten days later. The account given in the *Press & Journal* of 15 September was typical. Readers were told that many hits were registered and read breathless accounts of mast-top attacks in the face of ferocious barrages and of enemy ships being hit accurately while RAF bombers eluded enemy fighters. Claiming that the raid had 'struck a crippling blow at Germany's naval strength', the paper went on to inform its readers that the Ministry of Information claimed that British losses were 'considerably fewer' than the five aircraft claimed by the Germans on the day of the attack.

In fact, the raid had been largely ineffectual and had caused little damage at comparatively high cost. Fifteen Bristol Blenheim bombers had been sent to make low level attacks on the pocket battleship *Admiral Scheer* and the cruiser *Emden*, but five had failed to find the target in poor weather and had turned back. Of the remaining ten, five were shot down.[4] At least three hits were registered on the pocket battleship but none of the bombs exploded and the *Emden* suffered damage and some casualties only because one of the Blenheims crashed onto the cruiser. Meanwhile fourteen Vickers Wellington bombers had been dispatched to attack shipping which had been sighted at Brunsbüttel. Little is known of how effective, or otherwise, this attack was due to low cloud obscuring results. However, it seems likely that it was completely ineffective as only four crews claimed to have found a target to bomb and two bombs had in fact been dropped on the Danish town of Esbjerg, 110 miles north of Brunsbüttel, killing two people. Several of the Wellingtons were attacked by enemy fighters and two were lost.

Another early casualty was Master Charles Meston Milne (47) of the SS *Bramden*. Mr Milne was a native of Aberdeen and was the only son of the late Alexander Milne and Mrs Elizabeth Milne of 42 Brighton Place. In an adventurous life Mr Milne had gone to sea aged just 15 and had gained his Masters' ticket in 1915 before being commissioned into the RNR as a sub-lieutenant. He served throughout the First World War and at the conclusion of that conflict returned to merchant service. During the Spanish Civil War he had regularly journeyed to Barcelona and Valencia. Captain Milne had made his home in Barry, Glamorganshire, and left a widow, Ethel May Milne, a son (who was at sea) and a daughter. On 16 September the SS *Bramden* was in ballast, steaming from Dunkirk bound for Blyth when she struck a British mine and sank just off Dunkirk. The explosion was catastrophic and resulted in the

Captain Charles Milne. (Press & Journal)

entire aft deck being blown off and the ship sank very quickly. Despite the rapidity of her sinking there were only three fatalities, but Captain Milne was one of these. His body was washed ashore days later and was buried at Calais.

A further sign of the war was seen in the appeals for a further 600 Aberdonian blood donors to come forward in mid-September. Blood banks were established throughout Scotland (at Aberdeen, Dundee, Edinburgh, Glasgow and Inverness) and to maintain an adequate supply and stock at the Aberdeen site it was estimated that 1,500 donors would be required. Aberdeen surgeon William Anderson reassured Aberdonians that the work to set up the blood bank was going quite well but more volunteers were required very urgently, especially universal donors, so that the scheme could be completed as soon as possible. Therefore, he was organising teams of blood testers who would search for volunteers in Aberdeen and in towns throughout Aberdeenshire and neighbouring areas.

Another change which was immediately announced was that the government was to begin rationing petrol from 23 September. The scheme had been due to begin on 16 September but had been postponed for a week. This was sure to have a massive impact on businesses and detailed plans were outlined regarding the rationing system. For those lucky enough to privately own a motor vehicle the rationing would be extremely restrictive; motorists were urged to lay up their cars for the duration of the war and members of the public were immediately warned not to make unnecessary journeys.

In Aberdeen there were many people who were deeply concerned with the prospect of petrol rationing and letters to the local press and to the local author asking how special dispensation might be obtained were common. The press tried to tell people that the rationing would not cause the dislocation that many seemed to expect. Guides on filling out the relevant forms to request dispensation were widely available and after completion were sent to the local Divisional Fuel Officer, based in Dundee. The *Press & Journal* urged motorists with any queries regarding wartime motoring to write to the newspaper's motoring correspondent. Private motorists, however, were firmly warned that they could not expect any extra supplies of fuel to be made available to them as additional supplies above the ordinary ration would only be available in special circumstances, meaning that those who used private motor transport to travel to and from their places of work would have to rely on their ration and no more. Doctors were to be permitted enough extra petrol to meet reasonable requirements, while commercial travellers would receive a small extra ration, but this would not amount to what they usually had in the course of their business.

The private motorist had to apply for his/her petrol ration registration book at the City Motor Taxation Department at 24 Union Terrace (hauliers and other commercial users dealt with the fuel officer directly) and were informed that without their registration books motorists would be unable to obtain their coupon books. For private vehicles the ration system worked according to the vehicle's horsepower with petrol being classed in units, which were subject to modification at the government's discretion, as seen in the table below.

Petrol Rations for Private Vehicles

Vehicle Classification	Ration (units per month)
Motorcycle	2
Cars up to 7 hp	4
Cars 8-9 hp	5
Cars 10-12 hp	6
Cars 13-15 hp	7
Cars 16-19 hp	8
Cars 20 hp and over	10

The government had also decided that, with the harvest in full swing, the fuel rationing would not immediately apply to farmers with the proviso that when they were buying fuel they must be able to satisfy the supplier that they would be using the petrol for the purpose solely of agriculture and would have to sign a receipt for all fuel purchased. This exception also applied to vans and lorries that were operating under agricultural licences but, farmers were strictly warned, did not apply to private, personal, transport.

In the days leading up to the imposition of the petrol rationing system reports came in that some people were hoarding fuel by collecting it in drums and other large containers. Those who were considering this were sternly warned by the fuel officer that storing petrol without the necessary licence was an offence and that magistrates could impose a fine of £20 for each day the petrol had been stored.

One of the little, unheralded, dramas of the war to involve Aberdeen was the case of 12-year-old Irene Cooper of 46 Gerrard Street. During the summer a German woman and friend of the family had stayed with them and, after becoming close friends with Irene, had invited her to return with her to the Rhineland for a reciprocal visit. Irene's father, John, had agreed to the trip which was to begin in July and Irene was to return in September. The rising tensions between the two countries does not appear to have affected the thinking of either John Cooper or the family's German friend and when war broke out Irene was left stranded in the Rhineland.

Mr Cooper, unsurprisingly, 'was frantic with anxiety' and in his efforts to secure the return of his young daughter he approached the MP for South Aberdeen, Sir Douglas Thomson.[5] The MP in turn approached the US embassy for assistance and every effort was made by the embassy staff to secure the repatriation of Irene. Unfortunately, the German family with which she was staying were reluctant to let the child undertake the dangerous sea voyage back to Britain during wartime and the efforts to return Irene failed. She was forced to remain in Germany although Mr Cooper received several letters from his daughter through the Red Cross.

For the women of the Women's Voluntary Service (WVS) the first weeks of the war were extremely busy with many members helping to oversee the administrative functioning of a variety of important tasks including the evacuation programme, the organisation and call-up of ARP and civil defence workers and aiding in

WVS ladies at the Aberdeen City Centre WVS for Civil Defence Office. (Press & Journal)

the massive amounts of extra administrative work which was thrown up by the switch from peace to war. Many helped in the registration scheme whether as enumerators themselves or as administrative assistants, while others dealt with the paperwork for the forthcoming rationing scheme. Much of this work was undertaken from home or from rented offices, but that dealing with ARP and civil defence matters was largely carried out at the Aberdeen City Centre of the WVS for Civil Defence office. Without the strenuous efforts of these volunteers many of the early endeavours would have resulted in chaos.

For those who were attempting to ignore the realities of a Britain now at war their ignorance was jolted by the announcement that on 29 September every member of the public would be expected to enrol on the National Register. They would then be issued with an identity number and, crucially, an identity card. Without this card it would be impossible to obtain, for example, ration cards for petrol, food and other items which were to come under the rationing system. Scotland had been divided into 11,000 areas and more than 12,000 enumerators had been enlisted. The enumerators were each allocated an area and gave a schedule to every house, hotel, boarding house, school or other premises that might be occupied on Friday evening. It was then the duty of every head of household or community to fill in the schedule, on the evening of Friday 29 September, with the details of every person resident at that time. Details to be included were name, sex, marital status, occupation and whether the person was in any branch of the services or the civil defence services.

In addition to this, each person had to state if they had training in any other skilled job other than their current employment.

On the first day of October it was announced that all men aged 20-22 were ordered to register themselves with the military authorities for possible call-up. Prior to this, long lists of those occupations which had been classed as reserved had been published and many young Aberdonian men had already registered, but the announcement no doubt caused anxiety and was yet another sign that the war was for real. By the end of the month many young men were receiving military training. Those in the Reserves or the Territorials had been called up immediately and there had been a small surge of volunteers but, by and large, there was no rush to the colours as had happened in 1914. On 21 October men between 20-22 filed into the employment exchanges in Aberdeenshire and Kincardineshire to register for national service. Numbers were smaller than expected. In Aberdeen itself just 707 men registered, in Aberdeenshire and Kincardineshire the total was just 1,202. The main reason for this, according to reports, was that most of the men of this age group had already signed up to join the regular services or had joined the Territorials and been called up already.

As the Luftwaffe made a series of reconnaissance and probing flights to assess and attack military targets, the defences provided by the RAF received their first true test. On 8 October a Lockheed Hudson of 224 Squadron was patrolling the North Sea some 20 miles off Aberdeen when the crew spotted and attacked a Dornier Do18 flying boat which was engaged on a reconnaissance flight looking for British naval units or merchant shipping. The Dornier was shot down by the Hudson crew.[6] On the same day another Hudson from 224 Squadron reported sighting a small German fleet consisting of a battleship, cruiser and four destroyers. Unfortunately, bad weather meant that the sighting could not be confirmed or followed up.

With many Aberdonians being somewhat disgruntled with what we now call the Phoney War but at the time in Britain was largely referred to as the 'Bore War', in mid-October the people of Scotland received a blow to their morale when it was formally announced that in the early hours of 14 October the battleship HMS *Royal Oak* had been sunk while at anchor in Scapa Flow. The obsolete battleship had been struck by four torpedoes launched from a German U-boat which had somehow managed to penetrate the defences of the fleet anchorage. Amongst the 833 dead from the HMS *Royal Oak*'s 909-strong crew were two 17-year-old Aberdeen sailors. Boy 1st Class George Munroe Graham was the son of James Keith Graham and Ivy Florence Graham of 23a Forbes Street. Like many of those lost aboard the battleship his body was not recovered and he is commemorated on the Portsmouth Naval Memorial. The second victim was Boy 1st Class James Morrison. This young sailor was the son of William and Maggie Morrison of 538 Great Western Road, and, like his shipmate, is commemorated on the Portsmouth Naval Memorial.

The two young sailors had long been friends and had managed to remain together during their training in the Navy. Boy Graham was the oldest and would have turned 18 on 3 November while his friend had just turned 17 in August. They had been home on leave at Easter but had not seen their families since, though both families had hoped that they would be home for leave over Christmas and Graham's family had

Boys 1st Class
Graham (l) and
Morrison (r).
(Press & Journal)

been planning a late birthday party for him at Christmas. Graham had been educated at Skene Square and Rosemount Intermediate Schools and had enjoyed seasonal employment aboard both the SS *St Sunniva* and SS *St Clair* before he enlisted in the Navy.[7] Morrison had been educated at Newmachar and had lived in Aberdeen since the age of 14. The two friends had joined the training ship *Caledonia* at Rosyth and were transferred from there to the *Royal Oak* in June.

Another fatality aboard the *Royal Oak* was Able Seaman Walter Duncan Paterson (21). A native of Kintore, he had been educated at Kintore Higher Grade School before joining the Merchant Navy. Sometime before the war, however, he had transferred to the Royal Navy where he had been assigned as a gunner to the *Royal Oak*. Like his two crewmates, above, he also has no known grave and is commemorated on the Portsmouth Naval Memorial.

The parents of Able Seaman Samuel Borthwick (20) of 8 Seaton Drive no doubt feared the worst when they heard the news of the *Royal Oak* as they knew that their son was stationed on the ship. However, Mr and Mrs Borthwick were greatly relieved when their son was able to contact them to let them know that he was one of the survivors of the sinking. For Able Seaman Borthwick this was already his second fortunate escape of the war. Shortly before the outbreak of hostilities he had been serving on the aircraft carrier HMS *Courageous*, but he had been transferred just before the war began and escaped the sinking of the aircraft carrier on 17 September.[8]

Another Aberdeen survivor of the *Royal Oak* disaster was Surgeon Commander G.L. Ritchie of 7 Fonthill Terrace. He had been educated at Aberdeen University, where he graduated in medicine in 1914, before joining the RN shortly after graduation. During the First World War he spent a period attached to the medical unit of the Royal Naval Division and had been awarded the MC in 1916.

With the limited military action taking place, the majority of Aberdonian casualties in the first year of the war were from the RN and the Merchant Navy. The RN was desperately short of ships to escort their convoys at this stage of the war and a number of adhoc measures were put in place. These included the conversion of some merchant vessels into what were known as armed merchant cruisers. While they could be equipped with guns, often old ones, it was far more difficult to remodel a merchant ship to make it as hardy as a vessel which had been built for combat from the keel up. One of the vessels which had been converted to this service was the former P&O ocean liner SS *Rawalpindi*. Commandeered shortly before the start of the war, she was hurriedly converted and armed with six obsolete 6" guns and two 3" guns, beginning service as HMS *Rawalpindi* in October. Assigned to the northern patrol, she experienced early success when she intercepted a German tanker, but her luck was not to last. On 23 November she was investigating a possible enemy sighting in the vicinity of the Faroe Islands. The sighting was revealed to be the German battleships *Scharnhorst* and *Gneisenau*. The *Rawalpindi* signalled the position back to base before her captain took the decision to engage rather than surrender as requested, despite being hopelessly outmatched (he had no chance of outrunning the German ships). Within forty minutes the battle, such as it was, was over and *Rawalpindi* was sunk with the loss of 238 of her 276 crew.

The only damage to the battleships was minor splinter damage to *Scharnhorst* caused by the one hit which the merchant cruiser scored. At least three Aberdeen men were killed aboard the *Rawalpindi*. Sub-Lieutenant Alexander Mackie (27), RNR, was the son of James and Isabella and was a native Aberdonian. Commissioned Electrician Robert Main (27), RNR, was the son of Alexander and Mary and was from Torry; another Aberdonian, Second Storekeeper Sydney Edward Smith (33), Naval Auxiliary Personnel (Merchant Navy) was the son of William and Isabella and left a widow, Rose Gordon Smith. The bodies were not recovered and all are commemorated on the Liverpool Naval Memorial. Just five days after the loss of the *Rawalpindi* the Aberdeen-based SS *Rubislaw* struck a mine and sank in the North Sea with the loss of more Aberdeen men and the deaths continued throughout the rest of the year.

On 19 December the dangers to the men of the Aberdeen fishing fleet were made plain when the trawler *Daneden* failed to return from a trip. The news of the loss of the trawler was not made public until early in January 1940 but the tight-knit Aberdeen fishing community were already well aware of what had probably happened. The *Daneden* was in loose company with the trawlers *Strathalbyn* and *Star of Scotland* when they came under attack from an enemy aircraft. The chief engineer of the *Strathalbyn* related how on the night of 18 December they had been lying close together with three other trawlers. At first light the trawlers spread out and shot their trawls but about 10.50am an enemy aircraft dived from the clouds and strafed the *Strathalbyn* with machine-gun fire. The aircraft then dropped a bomb which missed, but the bomber turned back towards the trawlers and, seeing that the *Star of Scotland* was bringing in her trawl and would be a stationary target, made a bomb run on the vessel during which a bomb from the aircraft landed on her deck killing two crew members and wounding a further two. Deck hand A.J. Cowling (33) was a married Aberdeen man and the other crewman to lose his life was deck hand R.E. Page. The two men killed were both buried in Aberdeen after the trawler returned to port.

The chief engineer denied German claims that the aircraft had mistaken them for patrol vessels saying that it was plainly obvious that they were fishing. With the *Star of Scotland* wallowing, the skipper of the *Strathalbyn* used an axe to hack away her gear and steered away from the scene at full speed. The crew of the *Strathalbyn* clearly saw the German aircraft machine-gun the survivors of the *Star of Scotland* while they tried to climb into their small boat and the crew instead returned to the stricken trawler.

Shortly afterwards the crew saw the German aircraft circling a column of black smoke as if it was machine gunning something. It was obvious to the crew that a ship had suffered a direct hit and where there had been four trawlers there were now only three. Attempts to investigate and rescue any survivors were prevented as the German aircraft immediately machine-gunned and bombed any trawler which attempted to return to the scene.

The *Daneden* had set off on 11 December and had been coaled and supplied for a trip of twelve days, meaning that she would have been scheduled to return on or about 23 December. She had aboard a crew complement of nine men and all inquiries as to her whereabouts received a negative response. All of the crew were from Aberdeenshire with the exception of two men from Buckie in neighbouring Banffshire. The crew were: skipper George Bowie (39) of 2 Tullos Circle; second hand Thomas Reynolds (53) of 43 Summerfield Terrace; chief engineer James Morrison (55) of 1 Rosebank Terrace; second engineer James Broadfoot (64) of 109 Gerrard Street; fisherman James Bowie (58) of 76 Victoria Road, Torry; fireman George Tait (23) of Moray Road, Fraserburgh; deck hand James F. Geddes (28) of 69 Park Street (a native of Portgordon); deck hand William Paterson (36) of 32 Seatown, Buckie and cook William Reid (29) of 21 Bridgend, Buckie. The fireman, George Tait, was a late replacement as the regular fireman in the crew, Richard Mair of Main Street, Buckie, was injured and unable to go on the trip. The mate, Thomas Reynolds, had served as a skipper in the RNR during the First World War and had been awarded the DSM.

CHAPTER 2

1940 – Into Battle

By 5 January the *Daneden* was ten days overdue and there was much anxiety amongst the relatives and friends of the crew and the owners of the vessel. Exhaustive questions had been asked of other members of the shipping fleet but, it was claimed officially, no evidence had been forthcoming. The chief engineer of the *Strathalbyn,* who was mentioned in the previous chapter, could only testify that he thought that one of the trawlers in their group on that fateful day was the missing trawler.

By 10 January the trawler had been officially listed as having been sunk by enemy action and the crew declared missing believed killed. The skipper, cook, second engineer and both deck hands were married men. No bodies were ever found from the *Daneden* and all of the crew are commemorated on the Tower Hill Memorial.[1]

With the lull of the Phoney War the men of RAF Bomber Command found themselves being sent out on varied sorties including dropping propaganda leaflets over enemy territory and on long searches over the sea for enemy shipping, especially warships. On 2 January a number of Wellington bombers were dispatched on this task including Wellington IA (N2946) from 149 (East Indies) Squadron which took off from RAF Mildenhall but failed to return and was posted missing. The pilot of the missing aircraft was Aberdonian Sergeant John Morrice (28). Sergeant Morrice's aircraft had been seen over the sea but what had happened remained a mystery, although it was surmised that the Wellington had been attacked and shot down by an enemy fighter. None of the six-man crew survived and no bodies were ever found.[2]

On 15 May and with anxieties over the threat of an imminent German invasion heightening by the day, the government finally gave in to demands from all sections of the public and in the House of Commons to allow the formation of a citizen defence force to aid the regular forces in the event of such an invasion. That evening Anthony Eden gave a speech on BBC radio asking for men aged between 17-65 to put their names forward for service in the new formation which was to be known as the Local Defence Volunteers (LDV). Eden and the government had hoped for between 100,000–200,000 volunteers but the scale of the reaction took the government and others by surprise. Volunteers had been asked to submit their names at local police stations but the police themselves were completely unprepared for this and were quickly overwhelmed by the sheer numbers who came forward. As a result, the LDV very quickly began to organise themselves. This trend for self-reliance and dependence upon initiative was to continue to develop within the LDV, as an initial lack of uniforms, weapons, command structure and even a sense of purpose or list of duties, was overcome on a largely ad hoc basis which saw locally raised units mounting patrols with makeshift or borrowed weaponry on the very first night of their existence. In Aberdeen 600 men had enrolled in the LDV by the afternoon of 16 May.

Although the appeal had been very strict in its age restrictions the LDV also maintained a sense of initiative and self-determination and age restrictions were no different. While, nationally, on average the LDV age was in the mid-thirties there were many notable exceptions. Amongst them was Charles Hunter who enlisted in the Stonehaven Company of the 3rd Aberdeenshire (South Aberdeenshire and Kincardineshire) in 1940 at the age of 80. Mr Hunter paraded with the unit at its stand-down parade at Banchory aged 84.

While most LDV units were based according to their geographic location others formed around businesses or other organisations. The 6th Aberdeenshire (12th GPO) Battalion was formed from postal workers and was originally intended to protect Post Office assets in the event of an invasion. This was seen as essential as the Post Office sites included vital communication facilities which would be of great importance during an invasion. As the LDV and later the Home Guard developed and became both better armed and more efficient the role of the battalion changed and became incorporated into local defence schemes. Because of the nature of the 6th Battalion its companies were scattered across much of northern Scotland, although its headquarters and two of its companies, A and B, were based within Aberdeen. Other locations in which the battalion had companies, including three independent companies, were: Inverness, Invergordon and the Kyle of Lochalsh (C); Wick (D); Peterhead (E), Elgin; Kirkwall; Lerwick; Stornoway and Stonehaven.

With the German Army overrunning the Allies, including the BEF, the situation in France was disastrous and many Aberdeen families faced an anxious wait as the newspapers were somewhat remiss in reporting the events due to censorship; in many cases a positive slant was put on the news. In an attempt to stem the tide, the RAF mounted ever more desperate attacks on the German army. By 12 May the situation around Maastricht was dire and repeated attempts were made to bomb the bridges which the Germans had captured. The invaders, however, were well aware of the importance of these bridges and they were very well defended. As a result, RAF losses were very heavy. Early on the morning of 12 May two Blenheim squadrons, 107 and 139, were sent to bomb the bridges. No fewer than eleven of the Blenheims were shot down, amongst them was N6216. This aircraft was piloted by one of the squadron's flight commanders, Squadron Leader William Ian Scott, and took off from Plivot in the Marne Department of France at 5am but was shot down by ME 109s, crashing onto the west bank of the Maas; all three of the crew were killed. Squadron Leader Scott had flown on the Kiel raid at the start of the war. On this disastrous raid 139 Squadron lost no fewer than seven Blenheims and had fifteen men killed, two taken prisoner, while four evaded capture. Squadron Leader Scott was the son of Samuel and Margaret Scott and is buried at Rekem Communal Cemetery, near Maastricht. Although a Birmingham man, his parents lived at Aberdeen.

News of those posted missing after the fall of France continued to feed through as men were confirmed as having been taken prisoner or killed. With the loss of the 51st (Highland) Division a great many Aberdonian families were anxiously awaiting news. The 1st and 5th Battalions of the Gordon Highlanders were lost with the surrender of the 51st Division and there was tremendous anxiety in Aberdeenshire over the fate of the many local men who were known to be serving with that regiment. Such was the confused nature of the fighting in France during 1940 that, in the majority of cases where men were unaccounted for, the families were simply notified that their loved ones were missing and were forced to endure an agonising wait for further news.

Many families did not receive any news for several weeks after the fall of France and the surrender of the 51st Division. Some were erroneously informed that their loved ones had been reported killed, causing further heartache. In July, Mrs Jeffray of 50 Glenbarvie Road, Torry received the telegram that informed her that her son, Private R.S. Jeffray, had been reported missing in action. Two weeks after this the unfortunate Mrs Jeffray was informed that her son had been reported killed. Early in September, however, she received the 'joyful news' on 31 August that Private Jeffray was in fact alive, albeit lying wounded in a German hospital. The news came in the form of a postcard written by her son. Reflecting the confusion of the time, Mrs Jeffray received a formal letter on behalf of the King George VI and Queen Elizabeth expressing regret over her son's death just two days before her postcard.

Amongst the Aberdonian men who were listed as missing was Private John Morrice (21). An unmarried former farm servant, Private Morrice had enlisted in the Gordon Highlanders and was one of four brothers serving in the regiment.

Bomb Damage in Menzies Road. (Evening Express)

Victoria Road School in Torry. (Evening Express)

His parents received the news at their Woodside home at 27 Donbank Terrace. Finally, the family received the news that John had in fact been taken prisoner and was in a camp along with many other men from the north of Scotland. For his father, also named John, this must have brought back memories as he had himself been taken prisoner during the First World War.

In a number of cases there were multiple siblings who were taken prisoner during the fall of France. Amongst them were Corporal James R. Durward and Corporal

Pvt John Morrice (third from l, front row) in PoW camp. (Aberdeen Weekly Journal)

Arthur R. Durward of Stonehaven. The two brothers had joined the Army, both serving in the Gordon Highlanders, in 1934 and both were married. Their wives lived together at 40 MacDonald Road, Brickfield, Stonehaven, where they received the news of their husbands' captivity.

Another pair of brothers to be taken prisoner were Private Jack Hutcheon and Private William Hutcheon of School Croft, Balmedie. Both sons had worked for the County Council before the war and, once again, both were serving with the 5th Gordon Highlanders (as was another brother). William was single but Jack was married with his wife living at Scott Terrace, Belhelvie. For their parents, the news of their sons being prisoners was tempered by the knowledge that a further son, Archie, was still unaccounted for. Before embarking for France in January the Hutcheon brothers had been given a brief leave period to allow them to enjoy Christmas with their loved ones. The Hutcheon family were chosen to take part in a broadcast made by the BBC during which they reminisced and expressed the joy of having the whole family together for Christmas. Thankfully, it was later confirmed that Archie had also been taken prisoner.

Mr and Mrs G. Hunter of Park Crescent, Ellon, were anxiously awaiting the news of two sons, both serving in the Gordon Highlanders and missing in France. In late August they received news that one, Private John Hunter, was in fact a prisoner of war in Germany but his brother, George was still missing.[3] John had previously worked for Edinburgh Corporation.

The wife and two children of Lieutenant James Aberdein, Royal Army Medical Corps (RAMC), received news that he had been taken prisoner. The news would have been met with great relief when it arrived at their home at 142 Seafield Road, Aberdeen. James was well known in Aberdeen where he had taken an active interest in the Boys' Brigade movement and had worked as a radiographer at both the City Hospital and Woodend Hospital. Lieutenant Aberdein had served in the Territorials for a year before the outbreak of war.

Another RAMC man to be announced as being a prisoner was Sergeant Ernest Malcolm of 14 Margaret Street, Aberdeen. Sergeant Malcolm was married with a child and before the war he had worked as a partner in the Universal Window Cleaning Company. He had been a Territorial for two years prior to the war.

Lance Corporal Frederick Sibley had been a regular soldier for seven years and had seen service in India before the war. Called up to the Black Watch as a reservist on the outbreak of war, he had left his job as a motor salesman with the Kittybrewster Motorworks, Aberdeen, only to be taken prisoner after the fall of France. Lance Corporal Sibley was a married man with a child and had lived at 69 Broomhill Avenue, Aberdeen.

Private Stanley Taylor, Royal Army Service Corps (RASC), had also been confirmed as being a prisoner of war. Aged just 20, Private Taylor was the oldest son of the family and had lived at 8 Printfield Terrace, Woodside, with his parents. Prior to the war he had been an apprentice painter with the firm of Mr E.A. Copland and had been well-known in local football circles as he had played as a junior and a juvenile for Balmoral Thistle and Rosemount. Like many an Aberdeenshire family, the Taylors had more than just one son in the forces as Stanley had a brother in the RAF.

Above left: *Lieutenant J. Aberdein, RAMC, PoW.* (Aberdeen Weekly Journal)

Above middle: *Sergeant E. Malcolm, RAMC, PoW.* (Aberdeen Weekly Journal)

Above right: *Lance Corporal F. Sibley, PoW.* (Aberdeen Weekly Journal)

Below left: *Private S. Taylor, RASC, PoW.* (Aberdeen Weekly Journal)

Below right: *Private J. Hunter, Gordon Highlanders, PoW.* (Aberdeen Weekly Journal)

*PoWs and Missing
Aberdeenshire Men.*
(Aberdeen Weekly
Journal)

Pte. J. WHITE, Aberdeen, Prisoner.   Pte. J. JACK, Fraserburgh, Prisoner.   L/Cpl. W. FERGUSON, Aberdeen, Prisoner.   Sgt. E. MALCOLM, Aberdeen, Prisoner.

Pte. ALLAN WALKER, Aberdeen (Prisoner).   Dvr. W. G. DUNCAN, Aberdeen (Prisoner).   Pte. W. HUTCHEON, Balmedie (Prisoner).   Pte. M. CHRISTIE, Aberdeen (Prisoner).

Pte. ROBT. MELROSE, Aberdeen (Prisoner).   Sig. C. MILLER, Aberdeen (Prisoner).   W.O. W. G. ESSON, Slains (Prisoner).   Sgt. W. STABLES, Keith (Prisoner).

Pte. S. TAYLOR, Aberdeen (Prisoner).   Pte. THOMAS M'BEATH, Aberdeen (Prisoner).   Pte. J. WILLOX, Bucksburn (Prisoner).   Pte. G. WISELY, Bankhead (Prisoner).

Pte. C. S. FRASER, Elgin (Missing).   Bdr. J. LENNAN, Aberdeen (Died).   Cpl. J. M. DONALD, Aberdeen (Prisoner).   Flying-Officer GILLAN, Aberdeen (Missing).

The Sinking of the Lancastria and other Losses

As France fell and the situation became both increasingly desperate and chaotic, although the majority of the BEF had been lifted from the beaches at Dunkirk, there were still thousands of service personnel and British nationals in France. Desperately seeking a way to rescue them, the former liner RMS *Lancastria* (as HMT *Lancastria*) was dispatched to evacuate British nationals and troops from St Nazaire as part of Operation Aerial. By mid-afternoon on 17 June the *Lancastria* had embarked thousands of people (estimates range from 4,000-9,000) including civilians, troops (particularly pioneers and soldiers from the RASC) and RAF personnel. This latter group included a large contingent from 98 Squadron. Shortly before 2pm the Luftwaffe launched a raid and a nearby liner, the *Oronsay*, was hit on the bridge by a bomb.

Following this, and with the situation clearly becoming more urgent, the *Lancastria* was given permission to leave but the captain, despite advice from the RN, decided to wait until a destroyer escort was available. Shortly before 4pm the Luftwaffe tried again and this time the *Lancastria* was hit by four bombs causing catastrophic damage resulting in the liner capsizing just fifteen minutes later. German aircraft strafed survivors in the water and oil on the surface ignited. There were 2,477 survivors but thousands died, either drowning, choking on oil, burned to death or machine gunned in the water. Amongst the estimated 3,000-5,800 dead were a large number from 98 Squadron including Aberdonian Aircraftman 1st Class Patrick Gavin (19), the son of Francis and Ann Gavin. Like many of those who lost their lives during the disaster Aircraftman Gavin has no known grave. He is commemorated on the Runnymede Memorial.

For the anxious relatives and friends of those lost aboard the *Lancastria* their worries were increased as the government ordered a news blackout of the event but this was later broken by the Press Association.[4]

Lancastria *sinking after being bombed.* (Public Domain)

Lancastria *capsized and sinking*. (Public Domain)

Seaman Archibald Burness Petrie (19) of 28 Logie Avenue had been reported missing at sea on 29 June 1940 and his parents, James and Jemima, must have been going through agonies as they awaited news. Petrie had been aboard the Q-ship HMS *Willamette Valley* when she was sunk shortly after midnight on 29 June by a U-boat while 250 miles off the south-west coast of Ireland. There were only 25 survivors from the 92-strong crew and by early September Seaman Petrie had been listed as presumed lost at sea. His body was never recovered, and he is commemorated on the Chatham Naval Memorial.[5]

With its rich tradition of deep-sea fishing and close association with the sea many Aberdonians had either joined the Royal Navy or were called up for service in the Royal Naval Reserve. The Lees family were well known in the Aberdeen fishing community and one son, Andrew, had been a popular and well-regarded skipper before being called up for minesweeping duties as a member of the RNR. Younger son John Craig Lees (31) carried on with the Aberdeen fishing fleet. On 10 July he was a deck hand aboard the fishing vessel *River Ness* and was off the Skerries. The trawler, like many, was attacked and sunk by enemy aircraft with only two survivors from the ten-man crew, John was not amongst them and lost his life. Of the eight men killed at least six were from Aberdeen (it is highly possible that the remaining two were as well). They were: William George Davidson (18) of Torry, James Wallace Duncan (49), Ernest Garrod (25), Thomas Burford Hartley (57), George Peters Leslie (48) and John Craig Lees (31).[6] The news of John's death was delivered to his wife, Ethel, and his parents.

Just three months after John Craig Lees had been killed when his trawler was sunk by enemy aircraft, the Lees family received another devastating blow. Skipper Andrew

Robertson Lees had been captain of the minesweeping trawler HMT *Botanic* (FY 707) for just over a month when he lost his life during an attack by enemy aircraft.[7] Skipper Lees was one of six of the crew to be killed when a bomb hit the trawler. Well known in the fishing community, Andrew had served as a mate on board the trawler *John Morrice* as well as skippering several Aberdeen boats. He had been a member of the RNR for nine years and had been called up at the start of the war and from September 1939 until mid-July 1940 had served as skipper of the minesweeping trawler HMT *Dalmatia* (FY 844). He left a widow, Ann Buchanan Lees, at their home, 7 Brimmond Place.

Aberdeen Under Attack

The morning of 12 July dawned with a bright blue sky and the pleasant weather continued throughout the morning. Aberdonians were cheerfully going about their business or talking about the newspaper headlines of the morning which boasted of day-long dogfights over the south coast of England in which fourteen enemy aircraft had been shot down and twenty-three crippled by RAF fighters; the Battle of Britain was underway.

Aberdeen had been attacked on a couple of occasions in recent weeks and no-one had any doubt that the city, especially the shipyards and harbour, was a target for the Luftwaffe. At 12.45pm there came the terrifying sound of sixteen high explosive bombs exploding in rapid succession. Six Heinkel HE 111s from Stavanger had sneaked in over the North Sea and there was no warning for the people of Aberdeen before the first bombs dropped on the Hall Russell shipyard. Damage was severe and the boiler shop was destroyed when at least ten bombs fell onto it. Just outside the yard workmen were queuing to buy their lunch and the bombs took a terrible toll with many being killed. Those who rushed to the scene to help were met with ghastly scenes as many of the dead had been blown apart by the blasts.

The next place to be hit was the Neptune Bar where lunch-time drinkers, including more shipyard workers, were killed when a direct hit collapsed the building; the death toll here was also high. The manager later told reporters that just before the bomb dropped on the pub he was standing in the doorway and urged a man outside to take shelter with him. A second later the bomb exploded and the man was killed instantly. The publican was thrown across the room and struck his head on a picture which was a caricature portrait of himself. One of the barmen was badly cut by glass shards while several people in the bar and in houses nearby were killed.

In one of the nearby houses which was struck by a bomb a young mother, Mrs Tarburn, desperately tried to rescue her 21-month-old daughter who had been in her cot in another room. Finding the door jammed shut, she tried unsuccessfully to gain entrance through a window. A neighbour, Mr James Rose ran upstairs and managed to burst his way through the jammed door but found only wreckage. He then heard a child scream and this sound enabled him to rescue little Margaret Tarburn from where her cot was buried.

The bombing continued across the city with hits scored on the grounds of King's College, George Street, Regent Walk, Roslin Terrace, Urquhart Road and York Street. At Waterloo Quay the London Boat was also hit with further loss of life.

The sirens had sounded by now and people had taken to the shelters. The defences were also awakening with anti-aircraft fire sounding and a machine-gun mounted on the roof of the Station Hotel fruitlessly opening fire. Furthermore, a section of three Spitfires from 603 Squadron had been scrambled from RAF Dyce to intercept the intruders. As they approached the scene the Spitfire pilots, led by Pilot Officer Caister, saw that one of the bombers had become separated from the others and was heading out to sea. The Spitfires moved to intercept and turn the bomber back towards Aberdeen. Over the next few minutes a dogfight developed, during which the bomber jettisoned its remaining bombs, as the Spitfires jockeyed for a firing position while dodging return fire from the bomber's rear gunner. Hearing the chatter of machine-gun fire and the distinctive note of the Merlin-engined Spitfires hundreds of people emerged from cover to watch the dogfight. Finally, the RAF fighters got in a killing burst and the Heinkel burst into flames and began a slow dive towards the city below. As it neared the ground a wing struck a tree in Anderson Drive and the bomber crashed into the partially constructed ice rink causing the partly-built building to collapse in flames around the wreckage. A strong police guard was quickly put around

Wreckage of a Heinkel Shot Down Raiding Aberdeen. (Press & Journal)

the crash site while firemen battled to extinguish the flames. Despite the guard some eager Aberdonian boys still managed to approach the wreckage and secure some precious souvenirs from the German aircraft.[8]

At least 32 civilians were killed in the raid,[9] although contemporary accounts seem to claim far more lost their lives. The youngest casualty was 14-year-old George Lovie Webster while the oldest was 72-year-old James Robertson. Unusually, and probably reflecting the casualties including many shipyard workers, all of the victims were male.

Civilian Dead in Aberdeen Air Raid on 12 July 1940

Name	Age	Address	Notes
Allan Adam	42	30 Urquhart Rd	Hall & Russell
James Anderson	55	15 North Sq, Footdee	Hall & Russel (died in hospital)
William Leiper Baxter	22	27 Stafford Street	Hall & Russell, ARP
Gordon McKay Bisset	46	33 Union Grove	York Street
Peter Cable Chalmers	49	16 Ruthrieston Crescent	Hall & Russell
George Alexander Cromar	70	Matthew's Quay	York Street
James Currie	51	4 Loirston Place	Hall & Russell (died in hospital)
Alexander Davidson	66	2 Bannermill Street	York Street
Alexander Noble Geddes	40	14 Pocra Quay	Hall & Russell
David Gordon	42	8 Craigton Terrace	Hall & Russell
Charles Porter Gray	47	4 Girdlestone Place	Hall & Russell
Charles Greig	58	6 Powis Circle	York Street
James Ross Kinnaird	30	132 Don St., Woodside	Hall & Russell
William Leighton	66	88 Urquhart Road	York Street
Thomas Mulloy Leys	27	8 Kilgour Avenue	Died at Royal Infirmary
James Renoff Bruce McCoss	49	4 Rosehill Terrace	567 King Street (died in hospital), ARP Warden
William McKay	39	53 Tullo's Crescent	Hall & Russell
Hugh David John George McKenzie	59	2 Girdlestone Place	York Street
James McPherson	19	52 Mile End Avenue	York Street
William McTavish	27	72 Mansefield Road	York Street
Francis William Fisher Pirie	46	7 Seaton Gardens	York Street

John Pyper	41	74 Park Street	York Street
James Robertson	38	126 Rosemount Place	Hall & Russell
James Robertson (formerly James Imray Begg)	72	19 York Street	York Street
Norman McLeod Robertson	37	57 Logie Place	Died at Royal Infirmary
Thomas Dickson Sutherland	31	101 Commerce Street	Hall & Russell (died in hospital)
John Thomson	25	125 West North Street	York Street
Thomas Park Tosh	31	46 York Place	York Street
George Lovie Webster	14	9½ York Street	York Street
Ronald Milne Webster	26	86 Don Street	York Street
William Murray Webster	29	3 Firhill Place	York Street
Robert Williamson	17	183 Spital	Died at Royal Infirmary

Once again, early accounts of the raid in the press sought to downplay the severity and the number of casualties suffered, while lauding the response of civilians and the defenders. The *Aberdeen Weekly Journal* published on 18 July was typical of this reporting. The main story on the front page was about a raid on the north-east of Scotland and it described miraculous escapes along with an account of a bomber being shot down into the sea by Spitfires.

Another story featured the crash of the German bomber on 12 July. There was a strong reluctance to acknowledge the relatively high casualties in what had been a small-scale raid. Clearly the authorities still felt at this time that civilian morale might be eroded by news of casualties, but the operation of this policy which shackled newspapers was clumsy and undoubtedly counter-productive and led to a general distrust of official accounts. The account of the interception of the enemy bomber is typical of this. Readers were told that as the raiders were heard overhead 'Simultaneously Spitfires raced across the sky to intercept it. In a twinkling … the raider was at bay.' This implies that the RAF reaction was instant when, in fact, it was not, and the bomber was intercepted after bombs had already been dropped on the city; describing the bomber being at bay in 'a twinkling' was also an exaggeration. Most accounts agree that it took approximately six minutes for the three Spitfires to down the bomber after the initial interception, something which, in aerial combat, is actually a long space of time. Furthermore, this was a battle between three exceptional fighter aircraft and an already obsolescent bomber which was a straggler from its formation, possibly due to damage or mechanical failure. It may even, and this is supposition backed up by eyewitness accounts from the ground which all agree that the bomber had turned out to sea, have been tactically more sound to intercept the bomber as it tried to flee over the sea rather than force it to turn back to overfly a built-up area containing targets of military importance.

In the aftermath of the deadly raid questions were asked over the failure of the air raid sirens to give advance warning of the pending attack. Many of the criticisms were aimed at the Chief Constable. He responded by issuing a rather testy statement which stated that he was aware of 'wild statements which have been made throughout the city' but pointed out that it had been repeatedly stated in the press and on the radio that the responsibility for sounding the sirens was solely that of RAF Fighter Command and that he had no influence in the matter. Furthermore, he pointed out that the government had made the decision not to sound the sirens every time enemy aircraft were in the locality, a decision which local authorities across Britain were protesting against with vigour. Concluding his statement he informed the Aberdeen public that 'The Chief Constable is not in possession of any more information than members of the public as to the movements of enemy aircraft, so that suggestions which are being made that he can take action in defiance of those responsible are unsound.'[10]

The Birthday Honours List which was released in July included several men from Aberdeen. Lieutenant Colonel William Philip, Gordon Highlanders, was awarded the OBE. Having served with distinction in the First World War (where he was awarded the MC, mentioned in dispatches and wounded three times) he had risen rapidly through the ranks and had served in the current war. Renowned as a crack shot with a rifle, Colonel Philip was in business with his father in the Aberdeen firm of Messrs William Philip & Son, painters and decorators, at Alford Place.

Another OBE was awarded, this time posthumously, to Major Douglas William Gordon, Gordon Highlanders. Major Gordon (40) was the son of an Aberdeen timber merchant and had served with the Gordon Highlanders in the final year of the First World War before passing out from staff college and earning a position as a staff officer at the War Office. At the start of the war he had been military assistant to General Lord Gort before rejoining his own regiment. Major Douglas William Gordon, OBE, 1st Battalion, Gordon Highlanders, was killed in action on 4 June 1940 and is buried at London Cemetery and Extension, Longueval.

Lieutenant-Colonel W. Philip OBE.
(Aberdeen Weekly Journal)

The rush of wartime marriages continued unabated with many young women hurriedly marrying their beaus, many of whom were either already in the forces or were in the process of being called up. During the week of the air raid on Aberdeen a Rothienorman bride, Miss Lorna Kathleen Stephen, and a Lorgue airman, James Forsyth, were married at Auchterless Parish Church. The bridegroom was in the RAF but before the war had worked at the North of Scotland Bank at Strathdon.[11] The ceremony was

*The marriage of
Miss A.W. Stuart and Lieutenant
A.McD. Middleton.* (Aberdeen
Weekly Journal)

a simple one with the bride wearing a cyclamen coloured two-piece wool georgette suit. A rather more grand marriage ceremony took place at King's College Chapel, Old Aberdeen, when Miss A. Winifred Stuart married Second Lieutenant Alexander McD. Middleton. The young couple were both prominent members of the Aberdeen Lyric Opera Company.

As many Aberdeenshire families waited to learn the fate of missing loved ones the war continued unabated. The Battle of Britain raged overhead throughout the summer while other service personnel found themselves posted to theatres of war further afield. Such journeys were not without great risk. At the beginning of August, the converted troop transport the SS *Mohamed Ali El-Kebir* sailed from Avonmouth bound for Gibraltar with 697 troops from the Royal Engineers, Pioneer Corps, Royal Artillery, Intelligence Corps, Royal Navy and Marines, in addition to the ship's crew complement of 165. Shortly before 10pm on 7 August the troopship was sailing a zig-zag course 230 miles off the coast of Ireland accompanied by the destroyer HMS *Griffin*. A single torpedo fired by the *U-38* struck the troopship and she immediately began to settle by the stern. The escort chased off the submarine before rescuing 765 of the men who had been aboard the troopship. Amongst these were 549 of the troops. The troopship's master, nine crew, four naval personnel and 82 troops were lost in the sinking.

Amongst the Army personnel lost was Sapper Peter Sim of the 706th General Construction Company, Royal Engineers. Sapper Sim (30) was the son of Peter and Elizabeth Sim of 4 Perkhill Road in the village of Lumphanan. Before the war he had owned a shoemaker's business. His body was one of 33 later washed up on the

Left: *The Troopship*
Mohamed Ali El Kabir,
torpedoed and sunk off
Ireland. *(U)*

Below: *HMS* Griffin. *(U)*

coast of Donegal. He is buried at Kilcar Church of Ireland Churchyard, the only Commonwealth War Graves Commission burial there.

A second Aberdeenshire man from the same unit as Sapper Peter Sim was lost in the sinking of the troopship. Sapper John Fraser Garvock (29) was a married man who had grown up at New Pitsligo but before the war he had lived with his wife, Mary B. Garvock, at Peathill, Rosehearty. Unlike his comrade, Sapper Garvock's body was not recovered and he is commemorated on the Dunkirk Memorial.

Although the men of Fighter Command grabbed the headlines in the summer of 1940 the airmen in the other main branches of the RAF were also suffering significant casualties. Part of RAF Coastal Command, 233 Squadron was based at Leuchars flying regular patrols and anti-shipping strikes off the coast of Norway. This was an exceptionally hazardous task as the Luftwaffe may have been throwing most of its strength at the south of England, but it maintained a large number of fighter squadrons in Norway as well. Shortly before 9am on 31 July Australian Pilot Officer J.M. Horan and crew took off in Hudson I (N7224, ZS-O) for a patrol off Norway but were shot down into the sea by an enemy fighter. The four-man crew were all killed. Amongst them was Aberdonian Wireless Operator/Air Gunner Sergeant William Gray Cameron (21).[12]

Flying Officer James Gillan (26) was an experienced pilot having joined the RAF in January 1936 and seen service in Egypt and as an instructor in Canada. The son of an Aberdeen spirit merchant, he had been educated at Aberdeen Grammar School and then Aberdeen University. While at university he had established a reputation for himself as a keen golfer and played for the University Rugby 1st XV at full-back. He was recalled to Britain and served as an instructor at several units before being posted to 601 (City of London) Squadron on 3 August. This, the first auxiliary squadron, was one of the most unusual squadrons in Fighter Command and was widely known as the Millionaire's Squadron with many of its members flouting some regulations by, for example, wearing red socks and lining their jackets with red silk, but it had quickly established itself as a fine fighting squadron. The squadron was based at Tangmere during the first and second phases of the Battle of Britain (the phases were the convoy battles of 10 July – 7 August and the coastal battle of 8–23 August). On the morning of 11 August, the squadron's Hurricanes were flying a patrol off the coast of Portland when they appear to have been bounced by a force of Messerschmidt Bf 109s with the result that four of 601 Squadron's Hurricanes were shot down. All of the pilots were killed including Pilot Officer Gillan who was flying Hurricane I (P3783). Flying Officer Gillan has no known grave and is commemorated on the Runnymede Memorial.

Alongside the losses suffered in France those from the ongoing Battle of Britain mounted over the summer. On 5 September the *Aberdeen Weekly Journal* continued to publish lists which detailed the fate of men from the area. The first man to be listed was a veteran of the First World War. Corporal Allan J. Stewart (48) had served as an engineer in that conflict but in 1940 he was with the RAF and was stationed at Gosport where 17 (Training) Group, RAF Coastal Command, was based. On 16 August the Luftwaffe mounted heavy raids across the south of England. Early in the afternoon twelve Junkers Ju 88s, escorted by Messerschmidt Bf 110s dived to attack the base. Buildings were damaged in the attack and four people were killed. Amongst them was Corporal Stewart.

Stewart had spent much of his life in Aberdeen where his sister, Mrs Buyers, lived at 20 Hammerfield Avenue. At the end of the First World War he had joined the RAF and served for four years before returning to Aberdeen to work for shipbuilders Messrs Hall, Russell & Co. for several years after

Flying Officer James Gillan, killed during the Battle of Brtain. (Aberdeen Weekly Journal)

which he moved to London. Corporal Stewart was a married man with a daughter but, unusually, was buried near where he fell at Gosport (Ann's Hill) Cemetery.

The war not only saw large numbers of men join the forces, it also led to increased opportunities in the world of employment. By August Aberdeen was able to boast of record low levels of unemployment amongst men. This continued through September when it was announced that the figure for unemployed men stood at just 1,140, this compared to figures of 5,350 in September 1939 and 4,334 in January 1940. Throughout the year the figure had been steadily dropping as men either found employment in the wartime economy or joined up and by July there were just 1,816 unemployed men. For women, however, the situation was not so rosy. The year had actually seen the number of unemployed women increase as there were 1,754 unemployed women in September. This was an increase of 286 over the previous month, of 222 over January's number and of 91 over the previous September.

There was some excitement in Aberdeenshire when a Heinkel He115 seaplane crashed in bad weather at Windyheads Hill and men of the New Aberdour Platoon from the 1st Aberdeenshire Battalion of the Home Guard took the crew prisoner. This came at a time when the Home Guard were increasingly eager to demonstrate their capabilities and their use to the war effort.

The Home Guard suffered from a poor reputation amongst many members of the public who believed that they were doing nothing more than playing at being soldiers. The old nicknames of the LDV days such as 'Look, Duck and Vanish' were often repeated and this led to resentment amongst many who served in the Home Guard who felt that their sacrifices in the name of duty were not being appreciated. On 24 September a letter from General Sir John Burnett-Stuart appeared in the *Press & Journal* regarding the recent crash of the German seaplane. Sir John stated that it was shameful that the Home Guard did not get the recognition that it deserved and pointed out that in reports of the crash which appeared in the newspaper the claim was made that the situation was dealt with by the police with no mention of Home Guard participation. Sir John pointed out that this was wholly incorrect as it was a Home Guardsman who was first on the scene, who took the crew into custody and who reported the incident to his platoon commander. He then informed the police and took a police constable to the scene of the crash and mounted guard over the wreckage. Sir John pointed out that this was just the sort of incident for which the Home Guard was prepared when the presence of a single unarmed police officer might not have been sufficient.

Other Aberdonians found themselves facing an Italian offensive in the deserts of the Middle East. The RAF units in the area struggled with a climate which proved extremely taxing in maintaining aircraft, with lack of spare parts, obsolescent aircraft and a steadily dwindling supply of available aircraft. At 11.35am on 21 September Blenheim IV (T2061) of 14 Squadron took off, accompanied by two others, from Port Sudan to make a bombing raid on Otumlo airfield. The Blenheim was hit in the port engine by anti-aircraft fire and was unable to maintain flight. Flight Lieutenant N.G. Birks made a successful crash landing, but he and his two crewmen were taken prisoner. The gunner in the crew was Sergeant James Linklater Birnie Cheyne.

Sergeant Cheyne was a 23-year-old Aberdonian who, presumably, was injured in the crash landing as he died four days later.[13]

As well as training, patrolling, guarding and preparing themselves for a possible invasion, the men of the Aberdeen Home Guard also threw their weight behind various fundraising schemes. The Home Guards at Fetterangus, organised by section leader Mr Kell, held a free gift sale to raise funds for the Aberdeenshire Red Cross. The sale was opened by Lady Burnett-Stuart and was a great success with over £90 (almost £5,000 today) being raised for the cause.

One of the many problems faced by the Home Guard was the training of men in the weapons that they might be expected to use in the event of an invasion or raid. Many members of the Home Guard had, at the time, an ambivalent attitude towards these training programmes as they were being shown how to use sometimes advanced weapons but could see little sign of these weapons being issued in anything like the numbers that they had expected. In September, for example, Army regulars trained many Aberdeen Home Guards in the use of the Vickers medium machine gun.

An incident of heroism from a member of the Aberdeen Home Guard came to light in early October. James Craig of 18 Grampian Road was on night patrol when he heard two people shouting that someone had fallen into the water of Aberdeen harbour. Mr Craig immediately divested himself of his equipment before taking a rescue buoy and throwing it to the man. Unfortunately, he was too exhausted to seize the rope, so Mr Craig clambered down to the man and managed to loop the rope under his shoulders and then he and two other men pulled him from the water.

On 27 August the 15,007-ton armed merchant cruiser the HMS *Dunvegan Castle* was sailing between Freetown and Belfast when she was torpedoed off the coast of Cape Clear while escorting convoy SL-43. Hit by three torpedoes, the

*Home Guards
receive instruction
on the Vickers
machine gun.*
(Press & Journal)

Dunvegan Castle caught fire before foundering and sinking the next day. Of her 277 crew there were 250 survivors. Amongst the dead was Sub-Lieutenant Robert Gourlay Anderson, RNR (26). He was the third son of David Kinnear Anderson and Agnes Carruthers Anderson of East Gate, Laurencekirk, and had been at sea since he was 15. His two brothers in the Army had both been rescued from Dunkirk. His parents had been expecting him to return home on leave at the end of the month but instead merely received a telegram saying that he was missing, feared drowned. Sub-Lieutenant Anderson's body was later recovered and buried at Tullaghobegley Church of Ireland Churchyard, Donegal.

For many Aberdonians with an interest in aircraft the city's own auxiliary squadron, 612 (City of Aberdeen) Squadron, provoked interest and many followed its exploits as a member of Coastal Command. During the summer of 1940 the squadron had been flying anti-submarine patrols and convoy escort patrols using Avro Anson aircraft. They even used Tiger Moth biplanes to monitor the Scottish coast for enemy landings. The Anson, however, was not a suitable aircraft and in November the squadron was provided with Armstrong Whitworth Whitley bombers and began a lengthy process of converting to the new aircraft. One of the men who had been very involved in the setting up of the squadron was Squadron Leader Alan Milne Scott (26). The son of James and Nellie Scott of Inchgarth, Pitfodels, Squadron Leader Scott had been educated at Aberdeen Grammar School, Merchiston Castle and St John's College, Cambridge. He had then worked in London for two years before returning to Aberdeen to work with the family firm, Messrs James Scott & Son Ltd., becoming a director. He was well known in Aberdeen business circles and was well-respected and liked by his colleagues in the Auxiliary Air Force. He had joined the auxiliaries in 1937 and was promoted to the rank of squadron leader in January 1940.

On the night of 5 November Squadron Leader Scott was navigator in a crew on a familiarisation flight in Whitley V (P5064). The bomber took off from Kinloss but crashed shortly after take-off killing three of the crew, including Squadron Leader Scott. Described in the local press as one of Aberdeen's own airmen, Scott's body was brought back home for burial. The funeral took place on 9 November with the coffin being borne from his parents' home by sergeant pilots of the RAF, while RAF officers flanked the coffin as an escort to the waiting RAF lorry and other members of the service lined the driveway. The coffin was conveyed to the church and grave by the same RAF escort and after the funeral a number of RAF and Army officers (Squadron Leader Scott had also served with an anti-aircraft unit in Aberdeen before he was called up) saluted at the graveside.[14]

Sunday 17 November saw the city companies of the Aberdeen Home Guard mount their first church parade. Through word of mouth news of the event had spread and many Aberdonians turned out to show their support for the volunteers, with large crowds lining the route which led along many of the main thoroughfares before ending at the West Church of St Nicholas. In two columns the Home Guardsmen, led by bands from the Gordon Highlanders, saluted as they passed Lord Provost Mitchell outside the Music Hall. Alongside the Lord Provost on the saluting base was the commanding officer of the battalion, Captain A.S. Anderson, and several other

Wellington Road. (Press & Journal)

military officers. During the course of his sermon the Rev. C.P. Millar welcomed the men telling them that they were well named as they had come together to protect their homeland at a time when invasion seemed imminent. More than this, he told the men, they were guarding everything that their homeland stood for.

His Majesty's Theatre played host to the debut performance of the all-Army revue show performed by 'The Balmorals'. Made up of members of a Scottish Division

Lord Provost take the salute at Home Guard church parade. (Press & Journal)

which was touring Scotland on an eight-week tour, the performers, mainly amateurs, who varied from captains to privates, provided a very high standard of show to the sell-out audience. The material was mainly from professional writers but some of the performers had written their own material. The war was prominently featured. One act was a Shakespearian parody with Hitler as MacBeth. This piece was written by Lance Corporal F. Barker and he also starred in the role of the Führer. In other sketches fun was poked at staff officers, the pioneers, air raid wardens and the ATS amongst others. The show also featured a strong musical element with Eric Linklater's song *The Home Guard*, Alan Melville's *Swinging of the Kilt* (described as the Scotsman's reply to *There'll always be an England*) and a rhythm quartet which proved very popular. The quartet consisted of Corporal W. Commerville, Lance Corporal E. Playfair, Lance Corporal G. Clarkson and Lance Corporal P. McGuire.

Many clubs and other groups had taken the reluctant decision to place their activities in abeyance for the duration of the war but one which had decided to determinedly press ahead with their business was the Aberdeen Business and Professional Club. Holding their annual meeting in November, the outgoing president, Mr H. Oliver Horne, described what had been a remarkable and challenging year which had seen members have to come to terms with wartime conditions including new ways of doing business and new tax rates. Mr Horne expressed his admiration and astonishment that

The Hot Rhythm Quartet of The Balmorals.
(Aberdeen Weekly Journal)

the club had not only continued to meet, but that it had indeed strengthened since the declaration of war, having lost six members but gained sixteen over the course of the year. He was particularly pleased at the strong representation from the university and remarked that it was a feature of the club which enabled closer links between the university and the business community of Aberdeen. This feature, he believed, was very unusual in university cities and might even have been unique to Aberdeen. The meeting concluded with the new president, architect Mr J.B. Nicol, thanking Mr Horne for his hard work and dedication before presenting him with a replica of the president's badge.

Mr J.B. Nichol. (Aberdeen Weekly Journal)

Despite the dire situation that faced the nation some in Aberdeen were still more concerned over petty sectarian disputes. A letter appeared in the *Press & Journal* on 18 November backing a recent protest that had been made by residents of Towie over the appointment of Roman Catholic teachers in their school. The correspondent stated that he or she had noticed that the number of catholic teachers in Aberdeenshire was increasing and that this was 'to the detriment of Protestant children' as less time was spent teaching 'our Bible doctrine'. The writer maintained that there was unfairness being shown as Roman Catholic schools could reject teachers who were not of their own faith while Protestant schools had no such power. The correspondent went on, increasingly hysterically, claiming that since Scotland was a Protestant state its schools should be protestant too. Reinforcing this point the writer said that Scottish schools were 'our inheritance from our Reformation fathers' but that since their establishment 'Rome has crept in'. The correspondent believed that the Catholic influence could be responsible for the recent claims that scripture teaching was falling out of favour in Aberdeen and that this was a direct result of 'R.C. influence working stealthily in our Committees'.[15]

Others were concerned that supplies of clothing for those who had been bombed out were not being made available as easily as they should be. There was especial concern over the issue of winter clothing for children in Aberdeenshire, with several letters appearing in the local press bemoaning the lack of urgency that was allegedly being shown by the authorities. A letter in the same *Press & Journal* letters column as above was typical of these. The letter was from a W. Lowe of Elm Cottage, Montgarrie, Alford. The writer explained how they were Aberdonians but had been living in London when they were bombed out and took the decision to evacuate to Aberdeenshire as a family of three adults and seven children. Having lost many of their possessions during the bombing, they were dependent on the authorities to provide suitable clothing but had been granted only £20 to clothe and feed the entire family, meaning that six of the children were unable to attend school as they did not have suitable winter clothing. The correspondent claimed that they had tried every possible source for relief but were still left without bare necessities and that it seemed that 'so far as our wellbeing concerns anyone, we might as well be dead'. Clearly believing that the authorities were lax in Aberdeenshire, the writer concluded by warning that if Aberdeen was bombed as London had been, then residents might find that they were having to 'face realisation of vague promises'.[16]

The WVS Fruit and Veg Scheme and Other Initiatives

Following a press report on men from Aberdeen and the north-east of Scotland who were serving on minesweepers in which it was said that the thing the men missed the most was fresh fruit and vegetables, the women of the Aberdeen branch of the WVS determined to do their best to remedy the situation. For months the floor of their office at 130 Union Street was daily covered with sacks, baskets and boxes of vegetables. Mrs F.S. Anderson and her colleagues sorted the vegetables in the office before two WVS drivers, Miss H.M.E. Duncan and Miss A.M. Pittendrigh, collected and loaded the vegetables every day before taking them to a depot from where they were issued to the minesweepers. On some days the daily weight of vegetables transported was 800lb.

The idea for the scheme originated in several English ports but was taken up in Aberdeen by the regional WVS representative Mrs Moir-Byres and was met with immediate and enthusiastic support from all members. Over the few months that the scheme had been in action every sort of vegetable had been donated, while large supplies of plums were given when they were in season. The WVS explained how the scheme operated without taking any supplies away from the general public as each batch consisted of small gifts which would otherwise never have reached the market. The donors were Aberdeenshire and Kincardineshire residents who owned gardens, large and small, and who donated what they could spare from their own supplies. One well known, but unnamed, Aberdeen woman collected fruit and vegetables from her district weekly and drove them to the depot in her car and trailer. At the other end of the spectrum a maid working in a Deeside house was a regular donor who bought a small amount of vegetables each week and delivered them to the office.

Appealing for more donors, one of the WVS members, Mrs Beard, told readers of the *Aberdeen Weekly Journal* that any contribution no matter how small, even if it was just, for example, a single cabbage, was welcomed and that there was no doubt that the sailors were very grateful for the fresh fruit and vegetables.

It was not only the supply of fruit and vegetables which the WVS threw themselves into. The women volunteers of the organisation filled many vital roles during the war with members working in canteens, collection centres, salvage centres, organising charitable funds and in other capacities. The Aberdeen branch established a comforts depot at 37 Albyn Place. This centre collected wool for dispatch to the 444 work parties which had been established in the north-east of Scotland with the centre sending over a ton each week. The centre also received the completed woollen comforts and dispatched them to members of the armed forces and by the start of December 148,077 comforts had been sent. The Stonehaven Depot at Allardice Street

Ms K. Henderson, Ms I. Reid and Mrs Pender at the Comforts Depot. (Aberdeen Weekly Journal)

issued 6,890 garments and each week volunteers there were issuing 80-100lbs of wool to volunteer knitters in Kincardineshire. Both the Aberdeen and the Stonehaven Depots were staffed by members of the WVS.

Breakdown of Woollen Comforts Issued

Item	Number Issued
Blankets	1,745
Caps	2,691
Pairs of Cuffs	997
Pairs of Gloves	6,989
Pairs of Steering Gloves	3,341
Helmets	9,334
Pairs of Mittens	12,797
Pullovers	4,179
Scarves	14,979
Pairs of Socks	45,486
Pairs of Gumboot Stockings	3,514
Pairs of Sea-boot Stockings	1,401
Miscellaneous Comforts	40,554

The Comfort Depot was the hub of a large-scale operation called the Co-ordinated War Comforts Scheme. This scheme saw 16,000 women knit the 148,077 comforts which had so far been provided. This had required the purchase of 19 tons of wool. In its first year the scheme also distributed to north-east Scotland men and women in the forces 61,700 games and items of sports equipment and 22,600 books. The scheme had raised £21,756 during the year and had disbursed some £17,021 of this sum (78 per cent of the total). The vast majority of this had been spent on wool for comforts. The scheme was entirely reliant upon the work of volunteers with women, men and even children offering their services.

Expenditure Accounts for the Comforts Scheme, 1940

Item	£	s	D
Wool for comforts, etc	11,443	16	11
Games, radios, etc	1,710	6	
Red Cross Society for PoWs	3,000		
Depot expenses	437	11	2
Packing materials, transport, etc	185	16	4
Postage, printing and stationery	244	7	10

The books and games were stored at the Aberdeen Depot, under the control of Miss Lunan prior to issue, but had begun its existence in the Hardgate Drill Hall before relocating. Since it had been opened the scheme had distributed 22,697 books and 9,175 magazines. It had begun after the committee realised the extent of the boredom which often afflicted men and women who were stationed in unfamiliar and lonely parts of the country. Sports were also a very popular pursuit by those in the forces and the scheme had dispatched a lengthy list of sporting and recreational equipment.

Sporting and Recreational Equipment Dispatched by the Comforts Scheme

Equipment	Number Dispatched
Indoor Games	2011
Bagatelle Boards	20
Table Tennis Sets	22
Packs of Cards	659
Footballs	138
Rugby Balls	15
Pairs of Boxing Gloves	92
Badminton Sets	2
Croquet Sets	2
Sets of Outdoor Sports Gear	153
Jigsaw Puzzles	325

The scheme had also dispatched 201 wireless radios and had received letters of gratitude from men on board minesweepers, soldiers and airmen. Thirty-five gramophones along with 1,206 records and 126 musical instruments had also been issued under the auspices of the scheme. The prompt and generous attitude of the public in donating items allowed the scheme to send a wide variety of other items which might be of use to those in the forces. In addition to seven pianos these included: 63 deck chairs, 11 tables, 110 walking sticks, 154 pairs of boots, slippers and shoes, 13 overcoats, 3 Tilley lamps, 54 bedrests and trays, 50 razors and 703 miscellaneous articles.

In addition to these efforts the scheme also partly financed a travelling cinema for troops and its scrap metal salvage scheme, under the governance of Mr H.B. Aitken, had collected some 253 tons of waste metals. Mr Aitken had overseen the set-up of a number of dumps throughout the district and was responsible for arranging the transport of scrap from these dumps.

Following the evacuation of Dunkirk and the subsequent surrender of the 51st (Highland) Division, the organising committee had taken the decision to begin to raise a fund for the support of PoWs by the Scottish Red Cross Society. The fund had raised £4,197 but the task of maintaining its main duty, along with raising money for the support of PoWs proved too much and towards the end of the year the society decided to hand over the role of fundraising for PoWs to the Red Cross.

The various churches also made a significant contribution to providing comforts to those who were serving in uniform. With large numbers of sailors, soldiers and airmen present in the city, alongside Home Guards and ARP workers and even more travelling through Aberdeen to other locations, it was a vital and complex task to ensure that they had adequate facilities for rest and relaxation along with places they could go to purchase a hot meal or drink. A number of canteens were opened in the first years of the war with the churches, and especially the Church of Scotland playing a leading role. The staff of these canteens were mainly volunteers, many of them women who were already having to cope with all of the other challenges of managing a home and family in wartime Britain. During the first week of December a new Church of Scotland canteen was formally opened by Lord Provost Mitchell.

In early December a sergeant major in the Gordon Highlanders was awarded the Military Medal as a result of his extraordinary adventures in France. Charles Fullerton was a married man from the village of Udny and his wife had been informed in July that he had been posted missing after the collapse of France. Sergeant Major Fullerton, however, had managed to evade the Germans and reach a neutral country before making his way back to Britain, arriving in October. His wife, staying with her parents in nearby Pitmedden, said of the award that it was 'delightful news'.[17]

With the threat from Luftwaffe night raids the RAF was flying constant night patrols using a variety of aircraft as night-fighters; 219 Squadron had been flying in this role since the start of the war and flying Blenheims throughout the Battle of Britain.

Lord Provost Mitchell opened a new Church of Scotland canteen in December.
(Aberdeen Weekly Journal)

By December the squadron had re-equipped with the far more effective Bristol Beaufighter. The Beaufighter was a good aircraft but could be tricky to handle and on the night of 17 December Aberdonian Wireless/Radar Operator Sergeant George Mennie Leslie and his pilot lost his life while attempting to land at RAF Debden. Sergeant Leslie (29) had joined the RAF in June 1940 and seems to have been rushed into action, joining 219 Squadron at Catterick on 2 August. He was a married man who left a widow, Grace Duncan Leslie (nee Milne), and his parents, Andrew Petrie Leslie and Mary Ann Leslie (nee Milne), in Aberdeen.[18]

RAF Bomber Command had taken part in the Battle of Britain by bombing possible invasion ports, sustaining heavy casualties in doing so. By the winter the command was being used in a piecemeal campaign which was still aimed solely at military targets (although due to the inaccuracies of the force at the time some bombs undoubtedly fell on civilian areas) using relatively small numbers of aircraft. With the heavy bombing of several British cities including that of Coventry, however, the situation was somewhat altered and permission was given to undertake a far larger-scale attack on a German city. Mannheim was chosen as the target for the raid on the night of 16/17 December. It was mounted by 134 aircraft but was not a success as bombing was widely scattered over the city with little concentration. Three aircraft were lost but a further four crashed in England on return. Amongst them was Hampden I (X3063) of 49 Squadron. The Wireless Operator/Air Gunner on board the bomber was Sergeant Alexander Milne Wood (26), son of John and Williamina Wood of Aberdeen. It was believed that the bomber crashed in the English Channel, but no bodies were ever found.

Although Christmas provided some opportunities for relaxation it did nothing to take away the anxieties of those who had loved ones serving in action. William and Janet Ogston received the dreadful news that their son, Sergeant Douglas Ogston, 210 Squadron, RAF, had been posted missing believed killed just two days after Christmas Day. Sergeant Ogston had taken off as a gunner in Sunderland I (N9022, DA-B) from 210 Squadron's base at Oban to as part of a convoy patrol. Returning at 9.17pm to Oban Bay, the flying boat landed but struck an underwater obstacle which ripped out the

Sergeant Major Charles Fullerton MM. (Aberdeen Weekly Journal)

bottom of the aircraft and caused it to flip over onto its back. Nine of the ten men aboard were killed, while the second pilot was injured. Only one body was found and the remaining eight men, including Sergeant Ogston, have no known grave and are commemorated on the Runnymede Memorial.

CHAPTER 3

1941 – Defeat after Defeat

The devastating blitz on Clydebank in March inspired widespread shock and sympathy around Scotland. For Aberdonians, who were well used to being bombed, the news was doubly troubling and they rose to the occasion magnificently with highly organised schemes being immediately set up to raise funds and provide aid of all kinds for those who had been affected by the blitz. By the end of the month the people of Aberdeen knew that Mr and Mrs Edward McIlroy of 66 Ferryhill Road, Aberdeen, and their young daughter, Margaret, had been killed in the attack. The couple were originally from Glasgow and had gone back to that city to spend a holiday with their parents, arriving only hours before the blitz. The family were in the house of Mrs McIlroy's parents, Mr and Mrs McQueen, when it suffered a direct hit. All but Margaret (8) were killed instantly; Margaret was pulled alive from the wreckage but died in hospital. Neighbours told the press that the young family had left for their holiday 'as happy as schoolchildren' and were a very popular couple.[1] The news of their deaths cast a pall over the Ferryhill district.

We have already seen how the Hutcheon family of School Croft, Balmedie, had made a BBC broadcast about their family Christmas in 1939 when the three Hutcheon sons, Archie, Jack (35), and William, had been home on leave. Sent to France in 1940 with the 5th Gordon Highlanders, the three brothers had been taken prisoner of war following the surrender of the 51st Division. It must have come as a particularly hard blow to the family, however, when they received the news that Jack had died in captivity at Stalag XXA on 18 March at Torun, Poland.[2]

The modesty of many of the Aberdonians who were decorated for gallantry during the war is marked. A typical example of this modest hero was Chief Petty Officer William Kennedy, RNR, of 12 Ferry Road, Aberdeen. CPO Kennedy was awarded the DSM by King George VI at Buckingham Place at the end of March but was remarkably reticent about the decoration. He would not even tell his wife what he had been awarded the medal for and refused to go into details merely saying 'Oh, it was nothing' when pressed.[3] Kennedy was a very experienced seaman having formerly worked as a trawler engineer before serving for three years on a whaler which took part in expeditions from Leith to the Antarctic. He had been called up before the war and had served with distinction at Dunkirk.

As the Home Guard continued to develop it became obvious that one area in which it was lacking was in suitable medical provision in the event of its being called into action. Most Scottish units, those in Aberdeen included, found a simple solution in persuading local GPs to volunteer their services. Others, including the Aberdeenshire battalions, were fortunate in having a university medical school on their doorsteps and quickly made use of both staff and students. The 2nd Aberdeenshire Battalion went above and beyond in acquiring its medical officer. The battalion persuaded Professor Sir John Boyd Orr to volunteer for the position. Sir John (later Baron Boyd Orr) was a world-leading expert on nutrition and physiology and had served in the RAMC during the First World War.[4]

As the Home Guard developed it took on new roles in order to relieve regular troops from static defensive duties. During 1941 it was decided that the Home Guard would be the ideal solution, once retrained, to man coastal artillery and searchlight batteries. The training was largely welcomed and many Home Guard units in the Aberdeen area took over such responsibilities. Like many of their duties, however, there was some official confusion over the delineation of roles and many units found that instead of being retrained as artillerymen they were assigned as defensive infantry to regulars manning the batteries. Official attitudes amongst regular officers towards the Home Guard seemed to see the units as being available as a last resort to supply manpower or to undertake tasks which they saw as being beneath regular infantry. Thus, the commanding officer of the 542 Coast Regiment at Aberdeen wrote to his superiors reporting that the batteries at Aberdeen, Girdleness, Peterhead, Salthouse and Torry Point could accept platoon-sized units of Home Guard for use as defensive infantry and four of the batteries could use Home Guard units on the batteries themselves as they were undermanned. The battery at Torry Point was not suitable for Home Guard manning as its 6" guns were kept at too high a state of readiness to be manned by the part-time soldiers. In an addendum he also admitted that the Home Guard could also be used to man and operate the secondary armament of the Torry Point battery, consisting of 4.5" howitzers and 75mm guns.

Coping with Clothing Coupons

As of 1 June many items of clothing were also placed on the ration. For the weary housewives of Aberdeen this was just another part of wartime life that they would have to cope with. Clothing, cloth, wool and footwear were all amongst items to be rationed. In an effort to make things fair for all, the ability to purchase an item was judged not by price but by the number of ration coupons, with officialdom claiming that the 'dearest gown from the most exclusive West End salon or the cheapest frock from the humblest shop in Britain will both require the same number of coupons'. Everyone was to be assigned sixty-six coupons per year, while hats and infants' clothing (up to the age of four) remained off-ration, although wool for knitting clothing for infants was rationed.

The announcement of the new ration was kept secret until the very last moment so as to avoid panic buying and hoarding. The shoppers in Aberdeen on the Saturday night before the announcement certainly had no idea of what was coming. Drapers in Aberdeen remained closed on Monday 2 June in order to make arrangements to implement the scheme. Although the main reason for the rationing was to maintain supplies, a strong subsidiary reason was to curb the uneven geographic distribution of supplies of clothing that had resulted from population changes due to wartime conditions such as evacuation and movement of labour. A third aim of the scheme was to ensure parity and fairness in availability to both consumers and sellers. Thus, the scheme would mean that small shops would receive supplies on an equal footing with large department stores. No additional registration was required and purchasers were not limited to just one retailer. One beneficial result of the scheme was that production of clothing would actually see a slight increase in order to cope with the commitments that were in place under the rationing scheme.

The coupon system was complicated, however, with a specific number of coupons being allotted for different articles of clothing. The Board of Trade and local authorities urged people not to be tempted to rush to the shops to use their coupons and the public were repeatedly told that causing such a rush on the shops would be foolish as it would leave people with no coupons left to buy winter clothing when the time came. Therefore, people were urged to be frugal and to plan ahead for their demands and also told that trafficking in coupons was illegal, but that it was permissible for a wife to use her husband's book to buy clothing for him.

Suits or costumes made to order had to be surrendered unless the order was placed before 1 June and proof could be provided that work had actually been started before that date.

There were a host of exemptions to the scheme. For example, it did not apply to second-hand goods or to women using wool for comforts for the troops. For those people who had lost all of their clothing due to air raid damage, two years' supply of ration coupons would be provided, while those who lost some but not all would receive coupons commensurate with the losses.

Such had been the secrecy with which the scheme had been introduced that ration cards were not immediately available and the people of Aberdeen were informed that until special cards were issued, probably in August, they were to use the margarine coupons in their food ration books (they were replaced so that they could continue to purchase margarine) with each margarine coupon counting as one clothing coupon. Once the twenty-six margarine coupons had been used then the new clothing book would be issued.

For those making their own clothing, as they had repeatedly been urged to do, the purchase of cloth was made according to the width of material purchased and the quality. For example, one yard of woollen cloth 36" wide would require the use of three coupons, while a similar amount of cotton material would require only two. In a move which later proved unpopular and open to abuse, if an amount of material was measured and weighed and showed a fraction of a coupon then the total would be rounded up to the nearest number of coupons. To explain this rather complicated scheme a leaflet was issued which gave full details along with an appeal to the public which was summed up in the slogan, 'Do not buy more than you need, nor before you must.'[5]

One problem which had not been thought about was the case of evacuees where their parents were in the habit of buying clothing for their children in their own home district and sending it on to them. This would no longer be possible as the margarine coupons for the refugees were in the hands of those caring for them.

The previously mentioned Hutcheon family of Balmedie reprised their Christmas 1939 broadcast (which went out early in 1940) when they appeared on an 'absent friends' programme. During the programme the family, including Jack's widow, sent their best wishes to the two surviving brothers who both remained in captivity.

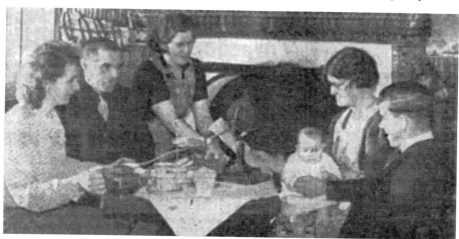

The Hutcheon family during BBC broadcast. (Press & Journal)

Bomb Damage on Aberdeen Beach, 1941. (Press & Journal)

Stell Road following Raid in August 1941. (Evening Express)

CHAPTER 4

1942 – Attrition

The Home Guard was becoming increasingly more effective and was now better equipped to play a far more substantial role in the defence of Britain. It was an essential part of local defence schemes but the liaison between the regular Army officers, who were in command of districts, and their Home Guard allies was sometimes strained by a reluctance on the part of regular staff officers to understand that the Home Guard operated far differently from the regular Army and that a different command style was required.

In February the commanding officer of the 1st Aberdeenshire Battalion, Lieutenant Colonel Sir John Burnett-Stuart, tersely replied to a request from his local zone commander (a position filled by a regular) for a detailed plan of his defence scheme, including substantial amounts of details including manpower and weapon strengths and positions. Lieutenant Colonel Burnett-Stuart brusquely informed the staff officer that the majority of this information was already available from the Aberdeen Sub-Area command and that as he had a headquarters staff comprising only himself, an adjutant and a quartermaster it was impossible for him to supply such complex documentation on a whim. The lieutenant colonel spoke, as did many Home Guard commanding officers, from a position of some authority as he had previously been a serving general, 'Director of Military Operations and Intelligence at the War Office, General Officer Commanding British Troops in Egypt and, prior to retirement, General Officer Commanding Southern Command and an ADC to the king'.[1]

As part of the defence schemes the Home Guard in Aberdeen received one very unusual piece of mobile equipment when the 4th LNER (Aberdeen) Battalion was given an armoured train. The 4th Battalion quickly passed on control of the train, named simply 'L', to the 7th Aberdeenshire (Works) Battalion, a unit which contained many railway personnel. The train was based at the depot in Inverurie but in the event of an enemy invasion or raid its action station was to be at Kittybrewster in Aberdeen. The train was relatively well-armed with its initial weapons load-out consisting of two Hotchkiss 6-pounder naval guns, a Vickers medium machine gun and four Bren light machine guns. It was based on an armoured and camouflaged GE 2-4-2 tank engine and a double-bogie tender which housed the ammunition supply. Along with the armoured train was a brake car and a passenger coach which transported the train's crew. This so-called mobile base was to be separated from the armoured train in the event of action, but still had its own defensive capabilities featuring a Boys anti-tank rifle and two Bren guns manned by its own crew of nine men (three train crew and six operating the weapons) under the second in command of the train and a company sergeant major (CSM). This meant that the train, commanded by a

Home Guard captain, boasted a full complement of thirty-seven officers and men. The weaponry was later upgraded by both official and unofficial means.

The 'L' train was allocated to coastal scouting patrols, providing firepower in required areas during an attack and to launch counter-attacks against enemy armoured units which were adjacent to railway lines. Another envisaged duty for the train was to help to destroy any enemy paratroopers who might land as diversions in the event of an Allied invasion of Western Europe. Although some assessed that the train (the 'L' train was one of three employed in Scotland by the Home Guard) would be of use in such operations, most Home Guards officers looked at the trains as being of limited utility.

The Warship Week Campaign

A civic banquet on 28 February opened the Aberdeenshire Warship Week campaign with the city of Aberdeen setting itself the ambitious target of £2,750,000 to fund a cruiser (HMS *Scylla*), while Aberdeenshire was aiming to raise a further £460,000, the price of a destroyer, and Kincardineshire £105,000, the cost of a corvette (neighbouring Morayshire was intending to raise the cost of a fleet minesweeper, £240,000). For Aberdeen to succeed in raising the £2,750,000 the daily average donations would have to reach approximately £400,000. The organisers informed the people of the area that the slogan for the next week was 'Every penny now!'[2] With the nation facing an unprecedented crisis, the necessity of funding the war effort had never been greater. Encouraging the people further they went on to state that as far as money in wartime was concerned 'it fructifies only in the Treasury'.

Speaking at the luncheon Lord Provost Mitchell stated that the task would not be an easy one, that his initial expectations had been to raise the sum of £2,000,000 but it had been decided to be more optimistic. Amongst the honoured guests was Rear Admiral Cantlie who stressed that command of the sea had never been more important and that although the Royal Navy had temporarily gained control at sea in the Far East, it was important to establish that control against Germany and for that more ships were needed.

Another guest, Lord Alness, handed over a cheque for £20,000 as a contribution to the campaign. He accompanied this gesture with the warning that 'the outlook is indeed sombre. There is no use pretending it is not. It is no time for shallow optimism; nor is it time for inspissated gloom.' The reverses suffered by the Allies, he went on, must serve as a stimulus for even greater efforts to get behind the national war effort. Lord Alness went on to offer praise for Russia claiming that 'Russia was fighting our battle … defending our coasts … was draining her life-blood that they and we might be free men and women. It was not too much to say that Russia to-day held the salvation of the world in her grasp.' He also told the audience that America was standing shoulder to shoulder with Britain and the two nations had developed a friendship which would outlast the war. As a result, he said, Hitler was forced to battle against three great democracies. Admitting that not all could fight, Lord Alness concluded saying that 'we can provide the equipment for the Navy, Army and RAF. I am confident that in the week to come the people of Aberdeen will be generous, even bountiful, and that this Warship Week will be a resounding success.'[3]

Local building societies offered a variety of plans which enabled people to contribute towards the various savings schemes such as Warship Week. For example, Equity & Law Life Assurance Society established a temporary office in Aberdeen, at 210 Union Street, for Warship Week. The society promised that a monthly payment of three guineas a week would instantly contribute £500 to Warships Week. This was done as the society would immediately purchase £500 worth of 3 per cent savings bonds which would be credited to an individual's Warships Week fund as soon as the first instalment was paid. At the end of thirteen years, or upon death, the savings bonds were transferred to the contributor or their representatives.

The main attraction on the opening day of Warship Week was a huge parade of service and civil defence forces through the city and a flypast and display overhead put on by fighter aircraft. Just before the start of the parade a flight of RAF fighters roared down the length of Union Street at roof-top height. Union Street's width made a perfect setting for the culmination of the parade when the columns saluted the Lord Provost and senior service officers at the saluting stand at the Music Hall. Those present on the stand were accompanied by a guard of honour and colour bearers carrying the White Ensign. As the first column neared the stand sailors ran up the signal 'SAVE' above the base.

A strong naval contingent, including RN, marines, WRNS and sea cadets, led the parade followed by a unit of Norwegians with their national flag, then artillerymen with their guns, soldiers from Highland regiments, ATS, Home Guard, airmen, WAAFs, and units of the ATC brought up the rear of the service parade. The civil defence parade contained a large amount of mobile equipment led by

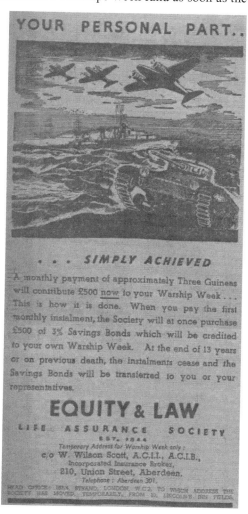

Equity & Law advert. (Press & Journal)

NFS motorcycle dispatch riders. Wardens in their newly issued uniforms, including blue berets, followed on from the NFS and all branches of the civil defence services played a role, with many female volunteers present. The parade was accompanied at all times by the presence of RAF fighter aircraft above. Spurred on by the events that had been organised and by the official encouragement, the people of Aberdeen took to the aims of Warship Week and on the first day alone some £561,800 had been donated.

The parade was very well received by an extremely large crowd which lined the route and only one incident marred the day. While the parade was in King Street a horse took fright at the sound of a pipe band near University Road. The horse was attached to a baker's van and when it bolted the 15-year old driver, George Lawrence Morrice of 27 Donbank Terrace, fell from the van and was later admitted to the Infirmary with concussion and head and leg injuries.

The local press threw themselves behind the campaign with gusto. On 2 March, for example, the *Press & Journal* featured a lengthy article by Vice Admiral J.E.T. Harper in which he described how vital the Navy was to the war effort and how 'Ships, More Ships, And Fast Ships' were needed to replace the recent losses which the Prime Minister had correctly defined as being 'most serious'.[4] The losses had been exacerbated by the recent events of the disastrous Battle of the Java Sea. The losses in shipping could well be, he went on, more serious to the outcome of the war than the loss of Singapore or the escape of the German fleet from Brest. Informing readers that 180,000 tons of shipping were being lost every month by the Allies, mainly merchant shipping which was vital for the supply of food and for moving men and materiel, the Admiral went on to say that these merchant vessels must be protected by warships and this was why the Navy was so vital to the war effort. Equally, reinforcement of the Navy would mean that greater effort could be devoted to surface attacks on enemy shipping.

The following day saw a plea for help in the Warship Week campaign by Rear Admiral C.G. Stuart. By this point the total raised stood at £1,053,923 7s 4d. Rear Admiral Stuart was opening an exhibition of naval, military and fire service equipment at the picture gallery of Marischal College. He urged the public to lend as

Members of the WRNS during Warship Week parade. (Press & Journal)

Right: Warship Week Advert.
(Press & Journal)

Below: Pipes and Drums lead Artillerymen during Warship Week Parade. (Press & Journal)

much of their capital as possible, insisting that they would get it back at a reasonable rate of interest. Urging donations, he said that it was 'up to everybody to spend as little as possible on amusements, and even on necessaries, and lend the money to the Government'.[5] The Navy, he said, was overstretched and needed ships 'very badly', therefore every donation, no matter how small, was important. The exhibition proved very popular with crowds coming to see the displays in the quadrangle which included a Fairey Swordfish torpedo bomber, a barrage balloon, a number of different anti-aircraft guns, bombs and mines. Inside the gallery were examples of smaller arms, including lend-lease guns from America.

The NFS had also made available a large display of some of its latest equipment alongside more antique fire-fighting gear. The RAF section was housed in the square room of the Music Hall and consisted of a wide variety of bombs (both British and German), bomb aiming and navigational equipment, a parachute and homing pigeons.

In the midst of the campaign the local press gave coverage to a rather fortuitous story featuring a recent investiture ceremony at which the king had awarded an Aberdeen naval officer with the CGM. Engine-room Petty Officer George Skene of 18 Young Street had worked as a trawlerman before the war but in the immediate pre-war years was employed at Aberdeen Fish Market. Whilst so employed he had joined the Territorials and at the outbreak of war was called up. Within weeks, however, he had been transferred to the RNR and during the Battle of Narvik in 1940 he was serving aboard a minesweeper and it was for his gallantry during the campaign that he was awarded the CGM. Although the local press covered the story in March there is some mystery as the award was not actually gazetted until 13 October. Naval bravery was nothing new to the family as his late father, Alexander, had served on minesweepers with the RN during the First World War and had won the DSM.

At the close of the week-long campaign Aberdeen had successfully raised the sum of £3,337,335 6s 8d. This was £587,335 more than the already ambitious target figure. One of the more unusual contributions to the effort was the donation of a Bible for HMS *Scylla* by the children of the primary department of West Church of St Nicholas. The children raised funds for the Bible and then used the remaining funds to buy savings stamps. There were also several very large donations made during the week. Leading the way were Aberdeen Savings Bank with £135,000 and Aberdeen Corporation with £100,000. The best single day in terms of donations was 3 March when over £861,643 was donated and the poorest was on the final day of the campaign, Saturday 7 March (Sunday 1 March did not count as part of the campaign) when just over £181,795 was raised.

Petty Officer George Skene. (Aberdeen Weekly Journal)

Day-by-Day Totals for Aberdeen Warship Week

Day	Date	£	s	d
Saturday	28 Feb	561,831	16	5
Monday	2 Mar	492,091	10	11
Tuesday	3 Mar	861,643	7	
Wednesday	4 Mar	313,435	12	8
Thursday	5 Mar	491,469	6	7
Friday	6 Mar	435,068	2	1
Saturday	7 Mar	181,795	11	

Large Investments made during Aberdeen Warship Week

Investor	Amount (£)
Aberdeen Savings Bank (Special Investment Dept.)	135,000
Aberdeen Corporation	100,000
Britannic Insurance Co. Ltd.	27,100
Standard Life Assurance Co.	25,000
Pearl Assurance Co. Ltd.	25,000
Scottish Amicable Building Society	20,000
Aberdeen Journals Ltd.	10,000
United Scottish Insurance Co. Ltd.	10,000
Aberdeen Northern Friendly Society	10,000
North British & Mercantile Co. Ltd.	10,000
Royal Aberdeen Hospital for Sick Children	10,000
Atlas Assurance Co. Ltd.	5,000
London, Liverpool and Globe Insurance Co. Ltd.	5,000
Guardian Assurances Co. Ltd.	5,000
London and Lancashire Insurance Co. Ltd.	5,000
Halifax Building Society	5,000
Sun Life Assurance Society	5,000
Norwich Union Fire and Life Insurance Societies	5,000
Commercial Union and Allied Offices	5,000
Eagle Star Insurance Co. Ltd.	5,000
Royal London Mutual Insurance Society Ltd.	1,500
Phoenix Assurance Co. Ltd.	1,000
Total	429,600

The organisers of the Warship Week were delighted with the response of the Aberdeen public and gave especial praise to the efforts of the small savers. By 13 March final

You'll like this new sweet

The sweet course is a bit of a problem to-day. But here's a recipe that tastes very good, is unusual, and doesn't need much sugar. It doesn't take long to prepare either.

Spice Pie

1 lb. carrots grated fine. 2 dessertspoons sugar. ½ teaspoonful mixed sweet spice. 1 heaped dessertspoon cornflour. 1 lb. short or potato pastry.

Put the grated carrot into a saucepan with the sugar and spice, and the cornflour previously mixed with ½ pint of water. Stir until the mixture thickens. Have ready a tart tin lined with crust, the edge well pressed up and fluted. Pour in the mixture and bake in a moderate oven until the crust is a golden brown all round the edge. Dust with nutmeg (if liked) and serve cold. (Enough for 4.)

Spice Pie Recipe. (Press & Journal)

tallies showed that the target total had been exceeded by £617,654 and that the final total raised by Aberdeen was £3,367,654 while Aberdeenshire had raised over £465,405, Kincardineshire £157,355 and Inverurie £26,035. The organiser of the campaign, Mr Forbes, expressed his sincere thanks to the people of the area who had donated so freely and generously. To demonstrate the determination of the people of Aberdeen to the campaign small free donations included £45 raised at a Cults coffee morning, £8 from a Ballater coffee morning, while Audrey J. Urquhart of 398 King Street raised 10s from raffling a tea-towel and Mrs Ross of 83 Oscar Road raised £2 by raffling a shawl.

Claiming that he was pleased with the results in Aberdeenshire, Lord Forbes also noted that the £465,405 10s represented an average contribution per head of population of £3 6s 6d. Lord Forbes admitted that this was 'still the lowest in the North-east' but that it was understandable given the fact that the weather during the week had been poor and that there had been an outbreak of foot-and-mouth disease during the week which had restricted movement for many people.[6]

Another feature of the Warship Week was that more people had taken part in the campaign than in any previous campaigns. Small savers had (without including the £135,000 investment by the Special Investments Department of Aberdeen Savings Bank) contributed £388,860 to the fund. The contribution of local schools had also been of great encouragement with the school penny banks producing £3,410 compared to £2,583 during War Weapons Week.

In this fourth year of the war and with rationing and the effects of the Battle of the Atlantic being felt very badly Aberdeen housewives were attempting find ever-more ingenious methods of providing tasty and nutritious food for their families. Providing sweet courses was a particularly knotty problem but the local press ran semi-regular articles on cooking alongside short recipes. In early March, for example, a recipe for Spice Pie appeared alongside claims that the recipe was tasty, unusual, did not require a lot of sugar and, crucially, did not take a great deal of time to prepare.

The chaotic nature of the fighting in Malaya had led to many delays in families finding out details regarding the fate of loved ones, but March saw two sets of brothers reported missing with the Gordon Highlanders. The first pair were Privates James and Charles McAllan of Aberdeen. James (29) had been with the regiment for eight years while his younger brother Charles (22) had joined in 1940. Their parents William and Jane waited anxiously for news only to hear that James had been taken prisoner, but Charles appears to have survived. The second set of brothers were from Longside. Arthur and Robert Morgan's parents, Arthur and Helen, lived at Chapel Croft. Arthur had been previously reported as being seriously wounded and it was confirmed that he had lost his life on 4 February. Once more, the remaining brother appears to have survived. The Morgans had two more sons in the RAF and a daughter who was serving in the ATS.

At the end of the Warship Week the committee were still reluctant to admit that the aim of raising £460,000 to enable the adoption of HMS *Somali* had not been the overwhelming success that they had hoped for. Late returns were still trickling in and then, on Saturday 14 March, a substantial contribution arrived from a London bank, donated by an investor who was connected with Aberdeenshire. This donation took the final tally to £460,125 1s. Despite the disappointment in just scraping the intended total, the committee did pay tribute to the 'people of modest means' who had managed to contribute over £40,000, more than they had managed in the War Weapons Week in 1941. Schools had made a significant effort in the campaign with Oldmeldrum raising over £2,211, Longside £1,000 and Alford over £400. The locally organised street groups also played their part with, for example, the Cults group raising £624.

One of the units to be based at RAF Drem in order to defend Scotland and the North-East of England was 210 'Cougar' Squadron, RCAF (Royal Canadian Air Force). In March the squadron was still equipped with the obsolescent Boulton-Paul Defiant night-fighter. During periods when the Luftwaffe was largely inactive over Britain the duties of the night-fighter crews could become somewhat tedious for young men, many of whom had joined up for the excitement of the war in the air. On the night of 16 March Defiant V1183 of 210 Squadron took off for what was noted on the log as a night-flying test over Northumberland. The crew consisted of Pilot Officer I.B. Constant and his gunner, Pilot Officer William John Lewis. The aircraft failed to return to Drem and it was later established that it had crashed in the grounds of Dissington Hall, Stamfordham, Northumberland killing both airmen. An investigation later established that the crew had been taking part in unauthorised low-level night flying manoeuvres and had experienced a high-speed stall which resulted in their fatal crash.

Pilot Officer Lewis had grown up at Rosebank, 17 Whitehill Terrace, Aberdeen, and had been educated at Robert Gordon's College prior to a pre-war career with

Pilot Officer William J. Lewis, RAF.
(Aberdeen Weekly Journal)

the North-Eastern Agricultural Co-operative Society at Bannermill Terrace, Aberdeen. At school he had been a keen sportsman becoming a leading member of the school's rugby team and later representing the Aberdeenshire XV. Obviously keen for some wartime excitement, he had volunteered for flying duties on the very first day of the war. Pilot Officer Lewis had two brothers in the Royal Artillery. One, Vic, was discharged after suffering injuries in Norway while the other, Arthur, continued to serve.[7]

Friday 19 March brought touching scenes at Aberdeen Joint Station as a number of Aberdeen women who had been rescued from Malaya as Singapore fell arrived home. Parents, relatives and friends were present in large numbers to welcome the women, but the reunions were tinged with sorrow as the women had left their menfolk behind as many had volunteered to stay back to aid in the defence of Singapore.

The women brought with them eye-witness accounts of the fall of Singapore and the attacks of the Japanese. Mrs McWilliam, daughter of Mrs and Mrs Bain of 32 Norfolk Road, related how their last glimpse of Singapore had been one of fires raging on the docks as Japanese aircraft launched a ferocious raid. Packed on board a ship they were then bombed by Japanese aircraft with several near misses. Mrs McWilliam's husband, George, had stayed behind. She told the waiting press that the first thing she was going to do was to seek out a job so that she could contribute to the war effort.

Mrs Greig's husband was John L. Greig, a former Aberdeen and University and Scottish International hockey player from Stonehaven who had been working in the Malayan government's agricultural service. Mrs Greig, an alumni of Aberdeen University, had heard nothing since of her husband but her attitude epitomised the spirit of the returning women.

Mrs Ogilvie's husband, Clifford, was manager of a tin mine at Ipoh and she was able to describe how at the outset of the Japanese campaign enemy aircraft had made low-level attacks machine gunning the town. Mrs Ogilvie had been evacuated from Singapore after retreating through Kuala Lumpur and Malacca. Her husband was the son of a well-known Torry doctor. The accounts of the women were, understandably, sometimes somewhat confused and Mrs Ogilvie made the erroneous claim that some of the enemy aircraft included German Messerschmitts.

Mrs Ruth Aitken, sister-in-law of the secretary of the Central Aberdeenshire Unionist Association, Mr H.B. Aitken, had faced an extremely long and arduous trek to Singapore. With her husband, John C.H. Aitken (who owned a rubber estate), she had escaped from the estate in Kedah near the Siam border when the war 'came suddenly and without warning'. The couple only realised the Japanese had begun the invasion when they bombed a nearby aerodrome.

The wife of another rubber plantation owner, Mrs Coutts, related how they had been amongst the last to leave. The plantation was on Carey Island near Port Swettenham and they were only able to escape via a narrow part of the river which they referred to as their back door. As they left the Japanese were bombing Port Swettenham. Mrs Coutts was the daughter of Mr James A. Meff of 48 Fonthill Road and a niece of the late Lord Provost Sir William Meff. Others who arrived at Aberdeen included Mrs Farquharson and her twin boys, Mrs Chalmers, Mrs Lamont, Mrs Winifred Davdson and Mrs Falconer.

Mrs Coutts (carrying overcoat) welcomed by Mrs Meff. (Aberdeen Weekly Journal)

Above left*: Mrs Falconer being Greeted by Mrs Kiki McKay.* (Aberdeen Weekly Journal)

Above right*: Mrs Ruth Falconer.* (Aberdeen Weekly Journal)

As we have already seen there was an ambivalent attitude from the regular Army to the manning of coastal batteries by the Home Guard and this continued through the early part of the year, but attitudes were changing. There had been movement with GHQ Home Forces ordering that all batteries should be provided with a Home Guard platoon of thirty men to act as defensive infantry but that 20 per cent of these men should be trained as gunners to replace regulars while further Home Guards should also be trained to provide cover. In June the regular Army manpower situation was providing some anxiety and there was further movement. Orders were passed along for either the closure of some Scottish batteries or their manning solely by Home Guards and rules were changed so that Home Guard batteries would receive priority in terms of recruits. By the end of September it had been established that the batteries at Girdleness, Peterhead and Wick (all under Aberdeenshire command) should be manned by Home Guards but that the battery at Girdleness currently had no Home Guard personnel at all and that a total complement of eighty-two was needed (two officers and eighty other ranks).

Even though the war was far from decided, the majority of people believed that a final victory would be the result and many were already turning their thoughts towards problems that might face Aberdeen in the aftermath of the war. There was undoubtedly a housing crisis in the city as bomb damage, combined with the slump in building which had accompanied the war, had resulted in a substantial shortfall in the housing market. At the end of June Mr Reginald Bisset of Messrs John Bisset and Sons, Builders, approached the Town Council with a proposal to open a factory which would construct and erect the new Tarran-type pre-fabricated homes. Mr Bisset was one of twenty contractors (across the country) who were sponsoring the Tarran homes and he claimed that if the type was approved by the government and the factory established then they could construct and erect 100 houses a week in Aberdeen. In order to do this the factory would employ approximately 1,000 people with only 5-10 per cent being required to be skilled craftspeople. Not only would this scheme ease the housing situation and provide 1,000 jobs, it would also guarantee the immediate futures of workers with other building contractors as they would be used to erect the houses across the city. The ambitious Mr Bisset also claimed that if the government authorised Tarran houses in more rural areas then the Aberdeen factory could be expanded to cope with demand spread across a 100-mile radius from the city.

While the Housing Committee worried about providing additional housing, the Electricity Committee was concerned that the increasing demands for electricity within the city would mean that additional plant was required to guarantee this supply. The electricity engineer was authorised to communicate with both the government and the North of Scotland Hydro-Electric Board in order to ascertain if any plans were already in place and to come up with a plan to cover the future needs of the city.

By 1 July it could be announced that the Aberdeenshire Salute the Soldier campaign had surpassed its target of £500,000 and that, on the fifth day of the campaign, the total stood at £572,483 14s 1d. Areas which had successfully broken their targets included Aboyne, Inverurie, Lower Deeside, Torphins and Turriff, while Kennethmont and Tarland had both tripled their original target and Kintore had achieved the third revised target that it had set.

On 20 September Aberdeen's adopted warship, HMS *Somali*, was torpedoed while escorting a Russian convoy. Most of the crew were taken off the stricken destroyer and she was taken under tow by her sister ship HMS *Ashanti*. On 25 September, however, heavy weather broke the back of HMS *Somali* and she sank. After the news was broken the people of Aberdeen decided to immediately try to raise funds for a replacement. In November it was announced that Aberdeenshire would participate in a four-month long campaign to raise £700,000 for a replacement warship. The destroyer which had been selected for adoption was HMS *Carysfort*, which had just been ordered.

The committee in charge of fundraising stated that the loss of the adopted destroyer had come as a blow to the people of Aberdeenshire, but that they could take great pride in the part which HMS *Somali* had played in her final mission and that the heroism shown would serve as an inspiration to the people of the district to ensure that the campaign was a success. Indeed, they reported, the 1st Belhelvie Girl Guides had anticipated the campaign and had already sent in a donation of £5.

The arduous and very dangerous training programme which was necessary for an airman to qualify for posting to an operational squadron took a great many lives. In October 1942 the trainee airmen of 10 OTU faced additional risks as, due to service exigencies caused by the growing losses in the Battle of the Atlantic, they found themselves assigned to the duty of mounting anti-submarine patrols, mainly over the Bay of Biscay, at the behest of Coastal Command. For this a detachment was posted to St Eval. On 29 October the crew of Flying Officer M.G. Grant took off in Armstrong Whitworth Whitley V (Z6579) for such a patrol. The dangers of these patrols had been increased as the Luftwaffe had posted 8/Jagdgeschwader 2 to patrol the area and the outdated and worn Whitleys were particularly vulnerable to attack. Flying Officer Grant's aircraft failed to return and the six-man crew were subsequently reported to have been shot down over France, lost their lives and been buried in Taule Communal Cemetery. It is very likely that the Whitley was shot down at 6.42pm by Oberleutnant Armin Landmann.

The second pilot of the crew was Aberdonian Pilot Officer William Ferries Raffan (25). Pilot Officer Raffan's parents, William and Margaret Ann, lived at 273 Rosemount Place while his pregnant wife, Margaret, was living with her parents in Osset in Yorkshire. After the war his widow and his parents had the following very poignant inscription placed upon his headstone: 'MAY THE WORLD REMEMBER AND ALLOW THE SON HE NEVER KNEW TO LIVE IN PEACE'.[8] The bodies of the six crewmen are the only Commonwealth War Graves in the cemetery at Taule and a plaque in front of the headstones reads 'To the Allies. Graves in the Field of Honour'.

Success for the 51st Division

There was a growing sense of pride in the resurrected 51st Division now playing a leading role in the successes in the desert. In December the workers at an unnamed Aberdeen munitions factory set themselves a target of producing a record weekly output in honour of the division. An article covering this placed a strong nationalist slant on this claiming that the southern English seemed surprised at the facts that the workers themselves had suggested the plans and that the Scots had come up with so many ideas to improve productivity. The writer claimed that harnessing local patriotism and a sense of competition would only serve to further boost productivity.

With the government recently claiming that the 51st Division was 'amazingly first in war', the writer claimed that Scotland could be proud. However, the writer was at pains to point out that there were famous English Territorial divisions as well, such as the 50th (Northumbrian) Division. He went on to say that it was unfortunate that governmental decisions had diluted the regional links with the Territorials during the conflict, but that local pride in regiments and other formations with local links could be used to boost production, especially in the area of munitions. The week-long campaign at one Aberdeen factory was admirable but, the writer argued, far more was needed with this war being very different to the largely static First World War. In this war concentration of power and speed of execution were vital to success. Somewhat surprisingly, the writer concluded by admitting that the Germans were masters in both areas and that, as of yet, the British had not yet excelled in them, but that every effort had to be made to achieve this goal. Reinforcing the claims that everyone was now on the front lines, he concluded by telling his readers that while the soldier must do the physical fighting 'the civilian must pass the ammunition as fast as human endurance will allow him'.[9]

The experiment in Aberdeen which had seen several factories linked with the name of the 51st (Highland) Division in order to bolster both pride and production was being keenly monitored by the government and it was thought that if the experiment proved a success that it would be adopted elsewhere in the country, especially in areas which were linked with particularly noteworthy military formations.

In the days before the fourth Christmas of the war many Aberdonians were thinking of how they might find some form of relaxation during the festive period. As ever the cinema was a very popular option and the highlight for many on 23 December was a personal visit to His Majesty's Theatre by Noel Coward followed by the showing of *Blithe Spirit* at the 2.30pm matinee screening. The theatre was showing three Noel Coward films over the next two weeks. These were *Blithe Spirit, This Happy Breed* and *Present Laughter*. The Capitol on Union Street was also showing a Noel Coward film, this time *In Which We Serve*. The Picture House was showing what is advertised as 'Merry Xmas Attractions' in the form of the Arthur Askey film *King Arthur Was A Gentleman* while the Majestic was featuring Vera Lynn in *We'll Meet Again* and a film called *Sabotage Squad*. The Tivoli, meanwhile, was presenting *Winter Revels* with Jack Radcliffe and the Odeon was showing *Sherlock Holmes and the Secret Weapon* starring Basil Rathbone and Nigel Bruce. For those who were more interested in keeping up with the war news there was the chance of a visit to the News Cinema on a Friday or Saturday where for the price of just 1s they could see two of the latest newsreels (including the topical 'The Fighting French'), a travel or interest film and a cartoon.

Above left*: Advert for Kinghorns.* (Press & Journal)

Above right*: Aberdeen Theatres for Christmas 1942.* (Press & Journal)

Others were more concerned with the traditional buying of Christmas gifts for loved ones and many Aberdeen shops had adverts placed in the local press to encourage buyers. For example, Kinghorn's on St Nicholas Street ran an advertising campaign in the days leading up to Christmas urging shoppers to 'Come and have a look around', promising useful gifts along with pretty and artistic presents and the store had a special Christmas window display to further encourage trade.[10]

CHAPTER 5

1943 – The Tide Turned

On 5 January, on the south coast, Private Alexander Greig (19), 2nd Battalion (London Scottish), Gordon Highlanders, and two other soldiers were assigned to strengthen a length of cliff-top defensive trenches. The three men went into a nearby forested area to gather wood, but one was ordered to report to HQ and shortly thereafter an explosion was heard in the wood. It was discovered that the three men had entered a restricted area and set off a mine. Those first on the scene discovered the body of Private George Robertson (18) of Orkney, but of Private Greig there was no sign initially until a search revealed a boot which had been issued to Greig. As a result, the young Aberdonian's parents, at 11 Seaton Drive, were at first informed that their son had been posted missing presumed killed on active service. An inquest held three days after the events heard from Lieutenant J.W. Slater that the men did not have to go into the area where the explosion occurred, and that it had been fenced off and danger notices were posted around it. The coroner stated that no inquest could be held into the probable death of Private Greig without a body being recovered.[1]

Towards the end of January two Aberdeen 17-year-olds found themselves imprisoned for committing deliberate acts of sabotage. The two, Thomas Barclay of 31 Danestone Circle and Marcus Pacitti of 119 West North Street, were employed at a factory in Ashgrove Road. The factory was engaged in what was described as essential work but, on several occasions, the two had removed vital parts of machinery, halting production on those machines. A foreman and a charge-hand both testified that on several occasions machines had been found stopped with parts missing and the two youths had been repeatedly warned that the matter was extremely serious and had been given the chance to replace the parts and restore the machines to work before the police were informed. Barclay pleaded guilty while Pacitti denied the charges. Two of Pacitti's former fellow workers were called to give evidence. Both had since been dismissed from the factory but denied allegations that they had in fact been removing parts originally as a practical joke but after becoming discontented decided to continue the sabotage in order to be dismissed. The managing director of the firm, Mr Alexander Wilson, under cross-examination said that he did not believe that Mr Pacitti was the instigator of the crimes but that he had been led into it and that he was under the impression that perhaps Mr Pacitti was being bullied.

Giving evidence, the police representative testified that after being cautioned the two youths had been taken back to the factory where they had produced a number of machine parts from a shelf and from behind a forge. On behalf of Mr Barclay, his solicitor told the court that both youths had behaved very stupidly but that they had not realised the seriousness of their crime or that it was an act of deliberate sabotage.

Passing sentences of fourteen days' imprisonment upon the two youths, Sheriff McDonald told them that he had taken into consideration their ages and the fact that they were obviously not the only persons involved in the acts of sabotage.

The end of the first month of 1943 brought tragic news to the family of Private Duncan Gibb (23). Hong Kong had fallen on Christmas Day 1941 but the fate of many of the men who had fought there was still unknown. Private Gibb had been serving with 2nd Battalion, Royal Scots and had been posted missing following the fall of the island. Towards the end of January Private Duncan's cousin, Mr G. Cummings of 143 Ruthrieston Circle, had received news that Private Gibb had lost his life and this news was passed on to the young soldier's parents, Duncan and Elizabeth. It was later revealed that the young Aberdonian soldier had lost his life on 11 December 1941.[2]

Problems in providing sufficient numbers of the Home Guard to man coastal batteries in Aberdeenshire continued throughout 1942 and into the New Year. The manning of a typical battery, it was estimated, required the presence of two regular officers, twenty-nine regular other ranks and eighty Home Guard other ranks.

The Home Guard in Aberdeenshire continued to expand and by February the University Company of the 4th Aberdeen Battalion had attracted sufficient interest to itself become a battalion and was renamed as the 9th (University) Aberdeen Battalion. We have also seen how the Home Guard in the city had come to rely upon medical students and staff from the medical school of the university for their medical officers and the new battalion took this a step further. The 9th consisted of three rifle companies and a specialised 'M' Company which consisted solely of staff from the medical school and medical students. 'M' Company's duties were very unusual in that in the event of an invasion or raid it was to place itself under the command of the director of medical services for the North Highland District and its members would be posted to a number of stations throughout the Highlands as medical officers.[3]

By early February the campaign to raise £700,000 to replace HMS *Somali* was at the half-way stage but, disappointingly, only £341,393 had been raised so far. The organiser of the campaign urged the people of Aberdeenshire to provide a late flourish and to ensure that the target was met by the close of the campaign at the end of March.

A further effort was made to ensure the comfort of merchant seamen who found themselves in Aberdeen. A Port Welfare Committee held its inaugural meeting at the Town House on 10 February with a view to dealing with accommodation, health, recreation and other factors which affected British and foreign seamen in Aberdeen. In order to, hopefully, ensure that relations between all interested parties went smoothly, there were representatives from the shipowners, trade unions, local authority, voluntary organisations and foreign seamen. The chairman, Mr Alexander Reid, told the meeting that the 'nation should realise that our ships and our courageous seamen are our lifeline'. At the conclusion of the meeting the Lord Provost also offered his support and commended the objectives of the newly-formed committee.

Although a great deal of effort had already been put into ensuring that there was suitable provision for the increased numbers of service personnel in Aberdeen, the Welfare Department of the War Office had identified one area in which the city was lacking. As a result a beautifully-panelled eighteenth-century house at 4 Castle

Terrace was loaned to the authorities by the Maternity Hospital and, after some remodelling, opened as a YWCA hostel for servicewomen and Land Army girls. Originally the house of a wealthy city merchant or the town house of a country laird, the hostel was quite opulent, featuring a large painting of a ballet dancer's dressing room adorning the wall of the recreation room. A yellow and blue paint scheme gave a cheerful theme to the twelve bedrooms, dining room, canteen and recreation room and several of the rooms featured other works of art. The facility was open to members of the ATS, Wrens, WAAF and Land Army girls and was formally opened on 11 February by Lady Helen Graham, the national president of the YWCA.

The fighting in North Africa continued to take a toll of Aberdeenshire men and late February brought news that impacted on music lovers in Aberdeen. Trooper Douglas Harry Mostyn Hoops (20) was from Huntly but was very well-known in Aberdeen music circles where his pianoforte recitals and abilities as a composer had won him many admirers. Before enlisting he had been awarded the ARCM by the Royal College of Music and had won the John Hopkinson Silver Medal. Trooper Hoops lost his life serving with the Headquarters Squadron, 2nd Lothians and Border Horse, Royal Armoured Corps. His parents, Douglas Evans Mostyn Hoops and Edith Amelia Mostyn Hoops (from whom he inherited his musical abilities), were notified at first that their son had been posted missing, but his death was later confirmed despite his body never being recovered. It would appear that he lost his life during the Battle of Kasserine Pass. On 21 February the 2nd Lothians and Border Horse were part of the 26th Armoured Brigade and they, with other elements from 6th Armoured Division were moved to reinforce the American forces with their mix of Crusader and Valentine tanks. It was on this day that Trooper Hoops was killed.[4]

Local RAF losses

As March began the commanding officer of the Royal Air Force, Sir Arthur 'Bomber' Harris, was preparing to put his main campaign against German cities into operation. He had been launching smaller raids to the Ruhr in order to fine-tune his tactics and to assess new bombing and navigation aids and on the night of 1/2 March he launched 302 bombers at the German capital. One of the pilots who had taken part in this operation, in which seventeen bombers were lost, was Sergeant Alexander Greig (22). Known to his RAF colleagues as Jock, Sergeant Greig was an experienced pilot flying Lancasters with 103 Squadron based at RAF Elsham Wolds. The squadron was in the doldrums as no crew had completed their tour of thirty operations in several months and losses had been high. Sergeant Greig and his crew were nearing the end of their tour, however, and many were hopeful that they would lay what was becoming to be seen as a jinx.

On the night of 3/4 March Bomber Command sent 417 aircraft to the coastal city of Hamburg. Unfortunately, the early Pathfinders made an error (using their relatively newly installed H2S radar sets) and most of the bombing fell 13 miles away from the city around the town of Wedel. The town was practically destroyed but, still, over 100 fires were started in Hamburg. Losses for the night were low with just ten aircraft failing to return (2.4 per cent of the force).

Sergeant Greig and his crew took off from Elsham aboard Lancaster I (W4788) shortly before 7pm. Along with his regular crew, Sergeant Greig had a second pilot on board on this night (known in RAF terms as a second dickie). Flight Sergeant James Mead (24) was going with Greig in order to gain his first experience of a Bomber Command raid before he would be allowed to take his own crew on operations. Nothing more was heard of Sergeant Greig and his crew and back at Elsham Wolds the crew were listed as missing. His parents, John and Margaret Esther Greig, were notified of their second son's failure to return from operations at their home, 7 Printfield Terrace, Woodside. It was later revealed that Sergeant Greig's Lancaster crashed at Hohenaspe and all aboard were killed. On 8 March the crew were buried at Hohenaspe and their bodies were later relocated to Kiel War Cemetery.[5]

On the day that Sergeant Greig and his crew were buried another Aberdonian airman lost his life in a flying accident while training in Britain. Sergeant Alexander Bruce Cowie (20) was an air gunner and was flying in the rear turret of Wellington IC (X3219) of 21 OTU. The crew of Sergeant Alexander McDougall (a 20-year-old fellow Scot, from Glasgow) had taken off from Moreton-in-Marsh on a night cross-country flight, but the aircraft crashed at 9.25pm. After hitting the ground at Barton St David, Somerset, the Wellington burst into flames and the five-man crew were all killed. Subsequent investigations concluded that the probable cause of the crash was engine failure but, somewhat mysteriously, the debris of the starboard engine was found to contain no less than 50 yards of wire. His parents, Alexander and Annie Guyan, were notified at their home, 12 Fonthill Road, that their son had been killed on active service.

On 16 March a massive crowd packed the Music Hall to hear an account of the defence of Malta given by General Sir William Dobbie. As the general took to the stage the entire crowd rose to their feet and burst into spontaneous applause to pay tribute to the courage of Malta. Amongst the crowd were men from the Army, Navy and RAF, alongside them were civilians from all classes. It was also commented upon that there were a large number of women and men of the cloth amongst the audience. The entire crowd sat in silent rapture as they listened to the vivid descriptions and imagined themselves on that embattled island.

After describing the early and dire situation on Malta (when the island's air defence consisted solely of four obsolescent Gloster Gladiator biplanes and sixteen antiquated anti-aircraft guns) General Dobbie once more brought the audience to applause when he assured them that Malta was now very strong indeed. The morale and attitude of the Maltese, said General Dobbie, was crucial during those early years as the Italians and then their German allies attempted to bomb the island into submission. The general kept the audience in rapture as he described how during the darkest days following the fall of Crete and Greece so few ships were getting through that supplies could be measured in days. Perhaps the most graphic of his descriptions to the audience was that of the saga of the aircraft carrier HMS *Illustrious*. He described how the dockworkers at Valetta had worked day and night to make repairs, despite repeated air raids targeting her, so that she might be seaworthy. On the final day the general was in a parliament meeting and could not concentrate as he listened anxiously for the wail of air raid sirens. He knew that the aircraft carrier was destined to sail that night for Alexandria if no further damage was done. After the sun went down the aircraft carrier put out and the workers' efforts were rewarded as she was able to make 28 knots and reached Alexandria. Upon hearing the conclusion to this story, the audience once more burst into sustained applause.

In conclusion General Dobbie paid tribute to the Royal Navy, the Merchant Navy, the RAF, the Army and to the Maltese people. An enthusiastic Christian, he added that tribute and thanks ought also to be paid to Almighty God for their success. Thanking the general, Vice-Admiral Raikes said that he fondly remembered serving with him in Palestine before the war, while Lord Provost Mitchell read out a note from Lieutenant General H.M.M. Crichton which described General Dobbie as a 'fine soldier and a Christian'.[6]

When Singapore fell in February 1942 the fate of a large number of Aberdonians, many of whom were serving in the Gordon Highlanders, remained unknown and worried families back home feared the worst as very little was heard and it was known that the Japanese often showed no mercy or consideration for those they took prisoner. Mrs and Mrs Alexander Anderson of Drumfrennie, Banchory, were one family anxiously awaiting news, nothing having been heard of their son since the fall of the garrison. Private Anderson was the sixth son in a family of thirteen and had joined the Gordons in 1933 and served in Gibraltar before being posted to Singapore. Amongst his large family were two sisters living in Aberdeen, Mrs Young at 511 King Street and Mrs Hutchison at 120 Huntly Street. After over a year of anxious waiting the family finally heard in March that Private Anderson had been confirmed as being a prisoner of war.[7]

The people of Aberdeenshire appear to have paid heed to the call for further donations to adopt a replacement for HMS *Somali* and by 20 March the total of £694,329 had been raised towards the £700,000 aim. As a result, nine days remained to raise the £5,671 that was needed. Sure enough, when the total sum was tallied it was found that the aim had been exceeded by almost £80,000; the total was £779,774 14s. The chairman of the county War Savings Committee, Lord Forbes, wrote that the success of the campaign meant that the *Somali* had 'been avenged'.[8] Lord Alness also wrote expressing his thanks to the people of Aberdeenshire for their support before expressing his confidence that the same support would be given to the forthcoming Wings for Victory campaign.

Throughout the war the police in Aberdeen had kept a firm eye on the levels of drunkenness in the city. In April Chief Constable McConnach made his annual report to the city magistrates. In it he claimed that the decision of some Aberdeen public houses to close for the half day on Tuesdays had resulted in a little extra custom for those that remained open but there was no overcrowding. Drunkenness in the city had been on the decrease for the last twelve months and McConnach attributed this chiefly to limited supplies, the decision of licence holders to restrict sales of spirits after 8pm and the shortage and prohibitive price of red wine. Assessing the spread of custom in the public houses and hotels of the city, McCulloch went on to inform the magistrates that pubs in the Market Street and Woodside districts, along with hotel lunge bars, were attracting the most clientele and that some were now very overcrowded, especially on Saturday nights. There were 263 licenced premises consisting of 136 grocers, 113 public houses and 14 hotels; a decrease of four compared to 1942. Cases of drunk in charge of a motor vehicle had also decreased, from 14 in the previous year to just 9 in the last.

Blitz on Aberdeen

For the men of the NFS, 20 April saw a visit from the Chief of Fire Staff and Inspector of Fire Services, Commander A.N.G. Firebrace. A display formed a key part of the day with fire-fighters demonstrating how quickly they could organise steel piping and hoses to supply water to an emergency site. The conclusion of the display was of a fireman on an 80' turntable ladder with a hose being fed at a pressure of 350 gallons per minute from a mobile dam. Commander Firebrace described the performance as extremely creditable and complimented Company Officer J.G. Pyle, the water officer, who was in charge during the exercise. During what was a short visit to the Aberdeen area Commander Firebrace also inspected the men of several NFS companies in Lower Deeside. Little did they know it but in just a few short hours the NFS men of Aberdeen would be confronted with the real thing.

At approximately 10pm on the night of Wednesday 21 April Aberdonians were shocked by the sudden appearance of enemy bombers overhead and the shattering sound of explosions rent the air. Dornier Do 217E heavy bombers of Kampfgruppe 2, based in Norway, had crossed the North Sea at low level approaching the city from the north-east, dropping their first bombs on Middlefield.

Dornier 217E. (Public Domain)

The raid opened with a small number of flares which lit up some parts of the city. Aberdonians who remained outside during the raid remember seeing tracer bullets streaking across the sky and some even saw raiders swooping down to spray machine-gun bullets and cannon shells into the streets after they had dropped their bombs. The districts of George Street, Hilton, Kittybrewster and Woodside were hardest hit, although bombs were scattered across other areas of the city too. A journalist with the *Weekly Journal* wrote of his experiences during and following the raid.[9] He had been on the roof of the *Journal* building on firewatching duty and so had a grandstand view. Describing the early minutes of the raid he relayed how at one point there was 'a terrific crash with a vivid yellowish flash of a remarkable width, as though a large number of bombs had gone off simultaneously'. These were the bombs which destroyed Middlefield School. The journalist believed that the raiders had been ordered to attack large buildings as well as densely populated areas of the city.

Incendiaries quickly caused severe fires and provided a guide for later bombers. In Hilton and Woodside, a number of bungalows and tenement buildings were simply wiped out while one bomber descended over Kittybrewster and dropped a bomb close to a shelter in which thirteen railwaymen had taken shelter. The impact of the explosion caused the shelter to collapse. Elsewhere in Kittybrewster bombs obliterated three bungalows and caused a tenement building to collapse

Bomb Damage at Middlefield School. (Evening Express)

with several families still inside. In the west end of the city a long line of bombs were dropped with one hitting the chancel of Carden Place Episcopal Church (the 'Tartan Kirk').

Causewayend Church was badly damaged by a bomb which blew off the front wall. At around the same time bombs fell on Gordon's College, a school at George Street and a night-nursery where several children received cuts and bruises. One of the most vicious incidents during the raid involved a Dornier which flew low over the city in circles constantly strafing any target it could see, including large buildings and heavily populated areas. This bomber at one point also attacked a bus with its cannon and machine guns.

Later in the raid the correspondent walked home and he described how the northern end of George Street was inaccessible and was enveloped in a sheet of flame while 'a dozen large fires seemed to stretch unendingly for about half a mile towards Split the Wind, throwing fantastic shadows among the wrecked or lurching houses'.

With the massive property damage, it was inevitable that a large number of Aberdonians were rendered temporarily or permanently homeless and

The ruined chancel.
(Press & Journal)

Above: Building Air Raid Shelters at Robert Gordon's College. (Press & Journal)

Below: Bomb Damage at Causeway End Church, 1943. (Evening Express)

the journalist reported how in many back streets he had seen straggling processions of such unfortunates, including many of the elderly and mothers with young children. These people were at serious risk as bombs continued to fall and enemy aircraft strafed the city. Nevertheless, the people of Aberdeen demonstrated great fortitude and courage as 'They flew to the rescue of neighbours buried in the wreckage of their homes. Sometimes they had to plunge to the ground as a raider roared over them and debris and bomb splinters whined above them.' In many of the harder hit parts of the city men who had already lost family members in the raid 'carried on heroically saving others whose homes had collapsed on top of them'.

Causewayend Church, 1943. (Evening Express)

Police, ARP personnel and firemen battled bravely to rescue people on George Street despite the bombs continuing to fall; their presence had a steadying effect in what was a chaotic situation but the 'linch-pin was the extraordinary courage of the general mass of the people'. The work of rescue parties and the ambulance service was made more difficult by the mounds of debris which littered the streets.

Many industrial premises, houses and the Royal Mental Hospital had been badly hit and at the latter site the Nurses Home was ablaze. Three fireguards were killed at the hospital and the Nurses Home was burnt out. The Meat Mart had also been hit by incendiaries, but the staff had managed to extinguish the fire using stirrup pumps. Houses in Charles Street were also well ablaze and not far away firemen were struggling to extinguish a blaze in a collapsed tenement, the ruins of which still contained families. A bomb had destroyed a nearby garage and feverish attempts were being made to dig out the thirteen railwaymen who were trapped in their shelter.

The Cattofield area was also badly hit with damage being caused at the Broadford Works, where the mill was destroyed, and at Sunnybank Primary School. The property of Ogston & Tennant Ltd, soap producers, was also hit. Half an hour or so into the raid two men had a lucky escape. They had sheltered in a doorway to watch the ongoing raid when they saw a plane coming straight at them firing as it did so. They dived into

Victoria Road School, 1943. (Press & Journal)

Cattofield following 21 April 1943 Raid. (Press & Journal)

the doorway just as an explosion blew them down the hallway, thankfully uninjured, despite the ceiling collapsing.

On the eastern side of the city many houses were left windowless after a stick of bombs exploded in St Peter's Cemetery. Three hours after the raid the journalist drove through Aberdeen and noted that the fires, which had raged out of control shortly before, were extinguished. The rescue and demolitions squads had continued to work throughout and upon making enquiries at the wrecked air raid shelter, found out that nine of the thirteen men had been pulled alive from the wreckage. There had been some amazing escapes. At one house only a single wall was left but of the four people who had been inside only one had been killed. Continuing his journey, he stopped beside the remains of a tenement building to speak with a police sergeant. The officer told him that they had rescued everyone from the tenement with seven walking wounded and three stretcher cases being removed from the building.

In neighbouring Bridge of Don twenty high explosive bombs and sixteen incendiaries were dropped. The Gordon Highlanders' barracks canteen was hit and 27 soldiers were killed while damage was also caused at D.C. Stewart's Yard, Joss & Sons Garage and the Grandholm Works. Several farms were also hit and there was considerable damage to dwellings, with ten families made homeless and foodstuffs destroyed.

Over the course of the short but sharp raid the 30 bombers taking part dropped at least 127 bombs causing very severe damage to parts of the city and killing 125 people with more than 200 injured. In one back street two elderly women had retired to bed and failed to take shelter. A large bomb detonating close by caused severe damage to the house and when the wreckage was cleared the two women were found to have been killed.

In the days following, stories of great courage emerged such as the Philips family of Summer Street and their neighbours, the Wilkens, who had run to their rescue. One unnamed man was seen calmly stemming the blood from a little girl's leg after she had been hit by a cannon shell despite the fact that bullets continued to hit the ground around them. The street fire guards had also acted bravely and it was said that between them they had extinguished no fewer than thirty fires.

One such fire guard was Frank Newman of 33 Charles Street. Mr Newman had only just escaped a stick of bombs which fell around him, when he found out that his house had received a direct hit. Upon reaching the house he found his wife, Barbara McBeth Newman (59), lying in the debris and he held her as she died. Next to Mrs Newman was the body of one of their daughters, Barbara (36), who was herself a fire guard. The bodies of their remaining three daughters, Mary Wemys Newman (26) and Isabella Newman (23), and a grandson, Ernest Shand Newman (4), were discovered in the wreckage. All of the daughters were fire guards. Despite his tragic loss Mr Newman continued to go on with his duties and took part in the rescue of two children from the ruins of a neighbouring house.

The stick of bombs which Mr Newman had escaped had exploded in Powis Place and Fraser Road and here the strongly-constructed surface shelters undoubtedly saved lives as no-one sheltering in them was injured and later inspections showed that the only damage was chips caused by splinters. The concrete surface shelters were of use against lighter bombs and blast, but heavy bombs exploding close by could result in severe damage or destruction. One surface shelter was blown clean off its foundations and thrown end over end. For those who were in possession of an Anderson Shelter even nearby direct hits could sometimes be survived. A policeman and his wife were in their Anderson at the bottom of the garden when a direct hit obliterated their bungalow. Although the roof of the Anderson collapsed the two emerged uninjured.

Bedford Road following raid of 21 April 1943. (Press & Journal)

The tenement buildings in working-class districts suffered badly with several of them being completely destroyed and collapsing on their shocked residents. Bedford Road was in a particularly hard-hit area and No.60 received a direct hit which destroyed the tenement which housed eight families. In a neighbouring tenement the ceiling collapsed upon a two-year old girl named Thomson. Rescue workers tried desperately to free the child, despite the continuing raid, but it was three hours before the child was successfully rescued. Her father and elder sister were also injured. In another tenement a young radio officer named Desmond Murray found himself trapped by debris which fell on his legs. The young man, who had just returned home from the sea on leave on 20 April, managed to extricate himself and on the morning after the raid was able to return to the ruins of the family home to help with salvage operations.

Fatal Casualties at Bedford Road

Name	Age	Location (Bedford Road)	Notes
Edith Annie Barclay	43	48	
Freda Gillan Cox	3	60	

John Forbes Gillan Cox	5 months	60	
Williamina Duncan Cox	22	60	
Ann Grant Duncan	43	77	
John Sandison Duncan	58	60	
Helen Davidson Grant	18	77	
Sheila MacKay	3	48	
William MacKay	38	60	Fireguard
Catherine Craigie Moir	43	60	Fireguard
John Mutch Moir	9	60	
Eileen Watson Paterson	18	77	
Alexander Anderson Porter	40	60	
Jessie Annie Wilhelmina Wilson	41	60	
June Lewis Porter	9	60	
Robert Alexander Porter	17	60	
Gordon Reid	15	48	
Robert Reid	10	48	
George Walker	18	75	First Aid Party
Isabella Craig Walker	46	75	First Aid Party
James Walker	53	75	
Christian Watt	70	60	
Elizabeth Watt	74	60	

During the raid police attended a bomb blast which had destroyed a bowling pavilion. Upon arrival they discovered the body of a man lying next to a bicycle and a spade. The unfortunate victim had been digging in his allotment and was on his way home when he was caught out in the raid. At one of the schools which was hit on this night a teacher on fireguard duty suffered severe leg injuries when two direct hits were scored on the premises.

ARP workers were always at great risk during air raids as their duties meant that they were exposed in the streets at the most dangerous time. At Hilton Drive a young ARP messenger lost his life. The messenger service was made up mainly of young boys and youths on bicycles who had volunteered for this dangerous but vital duty. James Hector Burr (17) was one such youth. The son of James and M.D. Burr, he lived with his parents at 100 Western Road, Hilton, and was killed while on duty at Hilton Drive.

At Stafford Street tenement residents took shelter in the basement but the building suffered a direct hit causing several to be trapped. They were rescued after a pet dog's barking was heard from above. There was a particularly sad story here as after the residents had been rescued and were in the street one man, William Webster (70), went back into the partially destroyed tenement to rescue the medals which he had earned in the Boer War and the Great War, but shortly after he entered a second incendiary hit the building and caused a severe fire in which Mr Webster was killed. As well as his medals Mr Webster also went back into the building to rescue his boots as he was barefoot.

Mr D. McKenzie was one resident who experienced a very fortunate escape. He was on his way to assist someone to a shelter when a bomb exploded nearby. The suction effect caused by displacement of air resulted in his being sucked into the resultant crater, but aside from cuts, bruises, shock and being winded Mr McKenzie escaped.

Mary Jack Forsyth (29) was at home at 20 Church Street when the raid began. Mrs Forsyth, whose husband, James, was in the Army, went upstairs to fetch her 16-month-old son when a blast ripped off the roof and cannon shells were sprayed across the property, killing both mother and son.

As usual the casualties were from all sections of society and were made up of all ages, although the working-class areas of the city were hardest hit. There were twelve victims aged 16 or below, including two brothers, Gordon (15) and Robert (10) Reid. The youngest victim was John Forbes Gillan Cox, who was aged just five months when he was killed at 60 Bedford Road. His mother, Williamina Duncan Cox (22), and his sister were also killed. Another youngster, 10-month old Kathleen Forbes was killed at 33 Brown Street, Woodside. Five children aged just 3 were also killed, they were: Angus Webster Brown who was killed at 119 Western Road, Hilton; William John Anderson Clark of 33 Charles Street; Freda Gillan Cox of 60 Bedford Road; Sheila MacKay of 60 Bedford Road and Evelyn Anne Calder of 6 Elmbank Road. The oldest known victim was Andrew Duncan (82) of 31 Charles Street.

We have already seen how five of the Newman family lost their lives, but there were many instances of entire families or several family members being killed. At 60 Bedford Road, for example, four members of the Porter family were killed, they were: Alexander Anderson Porter (40), his wife Jessie Anne Wilhemina Wilson Porter (41), their son Robert Alexander Porter (17) and daughter June Lewis Porter (9).

The journalist concluded his piece by saying that the people of Aberdeen had shown great resilience and had recovered almost immediately with the large numbers of homeless being quickly re-housed and 'Shaken, but still resolute. Aberdeen carried on.'[10]

Although this was true to an extent, it is the case that for many the night had been a shattering experience and many Aberdonians had lost loved ones, possessions or housing; all of this would take time to recover from. There were certainly those who remained obstinately defiant and in one windowless house the residents had flown a Union Flag and had their radio blaring patriotic messages. In some ways normal life did continue very quickly. Cattle sales were held on the day following the attack although the figures were low with a total of just 163 cattle being available for sale at the Central Mart. On the same day a sheep sale went ahead at Kittybrewster Mart where just 63 sheep were sold. Just days after the bombing pig sales in Aberdeen also went ahead at Kittybrewster Mart and Central and Northern Mart. In total 378 pigs were available for sale.

As the clear-up and search operations continued over the next few days, soldiers were brought in to assist the ARP personnel. This clean-up took some time as the devastation from the raid had resulted in a great amount of debris and had dislocated many services. It was not only the services who gave assistance to the authorities in the clean-up, however. Many civilians volunteered their own services and helped to clear the remains of their own and neighbours' destroyed properties.

In the immediate aftermath of the bombing many in Aberdeen and beyond came to the conclusion that this had been a raid which had deliberately targeted churches, schools and hospitals along with areas known to have a high population density.[11] The press quickly called the attack a terror-raid and published a picture of a ruined church under the headline 'Hun Desecration of Church and Homes'. Undoubtedly, this had been a terror-raid in the sense that its aim had primarily been to cause as many casualties as possible and to dent morale amongst the population of Aberdeen, but to claim that bombers at low level and flying at comparatively high speeds could accurately locate, identify and hit such small targets as individual buildings is surely an understandable, though false, impression. The Luftwaffe aircrew had undoubtedly

Rescuers clear away debris from a wrecked tenement. (Press & Journal)

been told to aim for large buildings and it was merely misfortune that so many churches and schools had been hit as a result.

For several days afterwards the Air Ministry claimed that the raid had been a small one undertaken by less than a dozen bombers and initially there was little information given out through official channels. Just two days after the raid, however, the authorities were forced to admit that the 'casualty roll is heavier than was at first believed'.[12]

By 26 April the local press had switched their focus to praising the stoicism and fortitude which was being shown by the people of Aberdeen. The *Press & Journal*, for example, cited the fact that a large number of church services had gone ahead as normal on the previous day, even at churches which had sustained serious damage. Members of the congregation took their places in one such church even though their service was in a building with no roof, a hastily constructed replacement altar and a piano instead of the destroyed organ. Some had brought flowers which helped to brighten the scene and the rector told the congregation that while they had lost property and buildings, the community had lost something far more precious in lives, including an entire family in one part of the city. In another bomb damaged church which stood amidst a neighbourhood where many houses had been destroyed and lives, lost the congregation observed a minute's silence for those who had died and in his sermon the minister praised the attitude shown by members of the community saying that there 'was never a murmur of complaint even from those who had lost everything, except what they stood in'.[13] In an attempt to raise morale and to boost church attendance in the wake of the devastating raid, the church bells were allowed to ring in Aberdeen and this was a move which was warmly welcomed by many.

A number of funerals for those who had been killed, including several for soldiers killed at the barracks, took place at the weekend and large crowds attended, lined routes and surrounded cemetery gates. The funeral for James H. Burr, the young ARP messenger who had been killed while on duty, was held with his cortege being led by uniformed members of the ARP services followed by those of the ATC, Army Cadet Corps and other civil defence services. His coffin was carried from the hearse to his grave by colleagues in the messenger service. At the graveside prayers were offered for all who were in mourning as a result of the raid.

For the many injured on that night the response of the first aid services and hospital staff saved many lives. Key to this was the blood transfusion service which had used 80-100 bottles of blood and plasma in the treating of victims. An official told local reporters that the service had undoubtedly saved many and supplies were still adequate. One of the more horrific aspects of the raid's aftermath was that the heavy blasts and fierce fires meant that the authorities were struggling to identify many of the casualties and an appeal was made for those with missing loved ones to come forward and give particulars to the police.

Sympathy from other communities also began to reach Aberdeen. Dundee's Lord Provost wrote expressing the profound sympathy of himself and all Dundee residents before saying that, although some aid had already been given, they were more than prepared to give more if it was needed. Meanwhile, the Lord Mayor of London wrote expressing his sympathy and placing the London Air Raid Distress Fund at the disposal of Aberdeen. Finally, Lord Rosebery, the Regional Commissioner for Scotland, had visited Aberdeen on 24 April and said how pleased he had been with the performance of the ARP and civil defence services and going on to express his admiration for 'the remarkable behaviour of the citizens'.[14]

One of the outcomes of the raid of 21 April was that Aberdeen Town Council reconsidered some aspects of its transport policy. Up until this point the city's buses and trams had not been suspended during a raid, with the decision of whether to run a service or not being left to the discretion of individual drivers. Following the evidence that at least one bus had been attacked by a German bomber during the raid, it was decided that in future raids transport services such as buses and trams would be immediately suspended and would remain so until the all-clear had been sounded.

With many Aberdonians' thoughts focussed on the recent air raid others had their lives torn apart by news that a loved one had been lost in action with the enemy. Helen MacRae was an Aberdonian who had married a soldier from Ross-shire, but as he was serving with the 5th Battalion, Queen's Own Cameron Highlanders, in Africa Mrs MacRae had taken the decision to return to live with her parents, Mrs and Mrs Duguid, at their home at 4 Gordon's Mills Road. Mrs MacRae received the devastating news that her husband, Company Sergeant Major Ian MacRae (21) had been killed in action.

Around the same time John and Emma Gordon of 27 Mansfield Place received news that their son, Seaman Dennis Gordon (18), had been lost at sea. Seaman Gordon had been aboard the SS *Chulmleigh* sailing from Iceland bound for Murmansk. The vessel ran aground on 6 November 1942 at South Cape and the crew took to three boats intending to make for Barentsburg (which was held at the time by a Free Norwegian garrison) some 150 nautical miles to the north. One boat had to be abandoned with the survivors crowding into the remaining two, but these became separated on the night of 7 November and a storm further hindered progress the next day. At this point several men began to die of hypothermia. One boat did manage to get ashore, but the survivors were not discovered until 2 January by which time just the master and eight crew were left alive. Seaman Gordon was not one of them, having died on 9 November 1942.[15]

The Women's Home Defence

There continued to be strong interest in membership of the Women's Home Defence in Aberdeen. Although the official government stance had shifted slightly to allow women to serve, it was with very strict limitations imposed upon such service and no chance of direct confrontation with the enemy. Women aged 18-65 were eligible to sign up for the Home Guard as auxiliaries but would only be permitted to undertake non-combatant roles such as clerical work, cooking duties and driving. The Women's Home Defence movement had been warmly welcomed in Scotland and Aberdeen had been no exception. Volunteers for the Home Guard had to be approved by battalion commanders and, although they would be able to resign at will, their commanding officers could also dispense with their services if they thought fit to do so.

Not everyone agreed with women taking a more aggressive role in the war. An opinion piece by Phyllis Bentley in the *Press & Journal* on 22 April (the day following the raid on Aberdeen) argued that the government policy was badly thought out as it was the natural instinct of a woman to fight to protect those she loved. Phyllis made the point that there were no female regiments, no female combat pilots and no women whose duty it was to attack the enemy. The women who were on anti-aircraft sites were tasked with engaging the enemy but purely in a defensive, not offensive, role. This, Phyllis claimed, was correct as a woman would defend but aggression was not compatible with a woman's temperament. Phyllis said that she believed that 'aggressive, offensive fighting' was 'inside the range of jobs suitable only for men'.[16]

Obviously the many Aberdonian women who had petitioned to join the Home Guard and who had formed the Women's Home Defence force would strongly disagree with this assessment and they continued to obtain unofficial training from members of the Home Guard.

Other girls and young women were turning their hands to more traditional (at least within 1940s Aberdonian society) feminine pursuits with the city finals of the Schools' Scottish Cookery Competition at the School of Domestic Science. The idea for the competition was that of the Secretary of State for Scotland and had been organised by the Scottish Education Department. All of the participants had been encouraged to pay particular attention to traditional and homely dishes of porridge, brose and potatoes and an array of dishes were prepared. The girls were given full scope for their own ingenuity in the creation of dishes which included oatmeal or

Women's Home Defence member receives training from Home Guard. (Press & Journal)

potatoes as the principal ingredient. The senior section resulted in a tie between Dorothy Duncan of Hawthorn Cottage, Methlick and Margaret Troup of 79 Leslie Terrace, Aberdeen. The junior section was won by Eileen Clark of 232 King Street, Aberdeen, while second place was tied between Betty Christie of 152 Victoria Road, Torry and Louise Kelman of 12 Esslemont Avenue, Aberdeen.

Amidst the more worrying rumours and claims made in the aftermath of the raid of 21 April was the common one that the anti-aircraft batteries surrounding the city had failed to adequately engage the enemy and, some people believed, had not fired at all. Possibly in an effort to refute these allegations General Sir Frederick Pile, C-in-C Anti-Aircraft Command visited the city on 18 May. Arriving by aircraft for what was termed a brief visit, General Pile, accompanied by numerous staff officers, undertook an inspection of the city's air defences before visiting the Lord Provost at the Town House for a meeting at which the District Commissioner, A.T. Morrison, and the Town Clerk, D.B. Gunn, were present. While General Pile had won great acclaim for his command of the country's defences, he found that at this meeting the Lord Provost was not best pleased and made a request for the strengthening of Aberdeen's anti-aircraft defences.

The Wings for Victory campaign

Aberdeen had already shown its commitment to raising funds for the war effort and the city was to hold its Wings for Victory campaign in the week beginning Saturday 19 June. This came shortly after the Dambusters raid (Operation Chastise) which had captured both headlines and the public imagination and it was expected that the campaign would arouse a great deal of enthusiasm. To ensure that it got off to a good start and to show how important it was, it was announced that the week-long campaign would be launched by the Chancellor of the Exchequer, Sir Kingsley Wood. The organisers set an ambitious target of £3,000,000 for the campaign, although they expressed the hope that they might even exceed that.

Sir Kingsley packed a lot into his visit including a tour of factories, savings banks, the Post Office in the city, followed by the North of Scotland Bank. While visiting Messrs J.M. Henderson & Co., an engineering firm on King Street, Sir Kingsley sat on a bench with four members of the works production committee asking them a variety of questions for some ten minutes before taking leave, wishing the men good luck and telling them to keep up their efforts. During the tour he walked among the machines and had a word of encouragement for the men and women in every department which he visited. Sir Kingsley seemed especially keen to give encouragement to the female workers. At Broadford workers cheered Sir Kingsley as he helped to empty one of the 'post boxes' which was being used by the staff as part of their efforts to raise funds for the war effort.

Sir Kingsley's next port of call was at the City Cinema where he was greeted enthusiastically by 2,000 children. While at the cinema Sir Kingsley presented prizes which had been won in the lettering and essay competitions organised for the Wings for Victory campaign.

After this hectic tour he gave a speech at a civic luncheon at the Douglas Hotel and then attended a parade made up of youth organisations including the Sea Cadets, Army Cadets, Air Training Corps, Girls Training Corps (GTC), Rangers and the pre-service section of the Girls' Guildry. At the Music Hall there was a large crowd who watched as Sir Kingsley inspected the honour guard formed by members of the ATC. Music was provided by bands from the Army, Home Guard and ATC while the music at the saluting base was provided by the RAF Coastal Command Band. The saluting stand was occupied by Sir Kingsley, the Lord Provost, service representatives, the heads of youth services and leading public figures from the city and county. After this Sir Kingsley moved on to a public meeting that night at the Music Hall.

Speaking at the public meeting on Saturday night Sir Kingsley spoke of his faith in the people of Aberdeen breaking the target figure. During his speech he said that his faith in Aberdonians had already been rewarded by their raising over £2,600,000 in War Weapons Week followed by more than £3,378,000 during the city's Warships Week and a further £530,000 for the Tanks for Attack campaign. This, he said, made a total of £6,520,000 but he wanted Aberdeen to now go one step better. One of the key ways in which fundraising efforts were so successful was in pitting communities against one another in friendly competition. Sir Kingsley demonstrated this when he said that he had recently visited Dundee and would be looking to see how both cities fared. The event at the Music Hall was not just a public meeting but

Lord Provost takes the salute during the Wings for Victory parade. (Press & Journal)

a variety concert. Music was provided by the RAF Coastal Command Band and by the choral singing of the recently formed Aberdeen WRNS choir. The concert was brought to a successful conclusion by a stirring finale including the display of the flags of the Allied nations.

One of the main attractions during the Wings for Victory campaign was the chance to inspect a Lancaster bomber (B for Baker) and a Hurricane fighter and large crowds attended for the opening ceremony of this event at Hazlehead. The guest of honour at the ceremony was Air Vice Marshal Raymond Collishaw who told the crowd that if they gave their support to the RAF the RAF would provide results. He went on to say that the intention was to end the war as soon as possible, before paraphrasing Winston Churchill telling the assembly that it was impossible to know if the war could be won solely by fighting in the air, but they were going to try. He went on to attempt to give the crowd some idea of how air power was growing all the time telling them, incorrectly, that a flying boat was being developed in the USA which could carry 50 tons of bombs, ten times the bombload of the Lancaster. It was also planned that, weather permitting, a Sunderland flying boat would fly over the youth rally which was to be held at Pittodrie Park on 23 June.

By the end of the first day of the campaign the figure of £292,869 had been raised although Lord Provost Mitchell could assure Sir Kingsley that over £1,000,000 had already been pledged.

Although the authorities urged people to remain at home during holidays thousands of Aberdonians ignored this advice in July to travel by rail and road. The sheer numbers placed great strain upon the rail network (which was why the government urged people not to travel) and the tail of the queue were only just able to board the final passenger coach of the final train departing for the south. The queues had lasted all day and at the Joint Station stretched throughout the station and out onto the street. On average people waited three hours for trains, queuing under posters asking people 'Is your journey really necessary?'[17] Queues for Dundee and Edinburgh were the longest at the station. A station official estimated that twice as many people were travelling compared to 1942. Meanwhile, large numbers of holidaymakers were entering Aberdeen with thousands of Glaswegians journeying north for their own holiday and, as a result, the station was reminiscent of pre-war July holiday weeks.

As a holiday-week treat a party of wounded sailors from the naval hospital at Kingseat were entertained at the Capitol Cinema. The men watched the film programme before being given high tea in the cinema café at the invitation of the manager. The outing was organised and made possible by the War Comforts Fund.

Despite the earlier claims that those who had been made homeless in the air raid of 21 April had been successfully rehoused, this was clearly not the case as a large number of complaints had been voiced revealing that significant numbers had not in fact been rehoused. In July a special committee of the Town Council was appointed and began to compile a comprehensive list of every unoccupied house in the city. Suitable houses were to be requisitioned by the committee which also heard about the existing practices for rehousing families and organising the repair of damaged properties.

Crowds at the Joint Station. (Press & Journal)

The Home Guard continued to take on more duties and this included the anti-aircraft defences of Aberdeen. This was a complicated job in which the Home Guard worked with members of the regular Army and with the many ATS women who also operated the batteries. At the formation of a new Home Guard anti-aircraft battery the Lord Provost inspected the men before ceremonially firing the first round from one of the unit's 3.7" gun before commenting 'It's lucky ma lugs were pluggit!'[18]

Not every Aberdonian was so keen on the anti-aircraft batteries. Some maintained that on the night of the blitz, 21 April, the anti-aircraft guns had failed to fire and this caused some lasting anger across the city. This was not true, but the rumours obviously continued to rankle and a defensive message from the officer responsible for the anti-aircraft defences of the city was relayed at a meeting of the Rotary Club in the Caledonian Hotel on 3 August.

The unnamed officer, who had only taken command after the blitz, was at pains to point out that the first duty of the anti-aircraft batteries was to protect material and key installations in the area and that they did this. He also made the claim that British anti-aircraft technology was 'miles and miles ahead of any other in the world'. He went on to relay something he had overheard a hotel porter say when he first arrived in Aberdeen. The man was berating the anti-aircraft units and said that if a machine gun had been mounted on every tall building in the city the entire raiding force could have been shot down. While remarking that it was a grand idea, he pointed out that it was unfeasible as the guns could not be manned at all times while a raider might never even come into range of such a weapon.

Answering the claim that the guns had failed to fire, he said that this was completely untrue and that far from failing to engage the enemy the gunners had on that night 'put up what was almost a record number of rounds' before stating, rather confusingly, 'We never hit any of the planes. They never hit us', before once again stressing that the duty of the batteries was to protect important sites rather than, it seems, the city as a whole. Rather tactlessly the officer then went on to say that 'Probably some of your houses were hit … but we stopped them from hitting the installations they were after. I know the feelings of civilians. I have had it before. If a house, the local cinema, or worse, the local pub is hit, they come and call us all sort of funny names and won't serve us with cigarettes or anything.' Amongst those defending Aberdeen on the night of the blitz were women of the ATS who were operating gunsights, predictors and rangefinders at several of the anti-aircraft batteries ringing the city. Defending the units under his command, however, he added that the women of the ATS had never batted an eyelid during the attack and had behaved superbly, adding, 'we really do our job. Unfortunately we did not knock any of them down … But the Commander-in-Chief himself came up and patted the gunners and the girls on the back.'[19] He did admit, however, that the Lord Provost had spoken with the C-in-C and had secured an agreement that the defences of the city be strengthened.

Thanking the officer, the Commandant of the Observer Corps, Mr G.M. Williamson, agreed with the officer saying that the gunners did not count an enemy aircraft as destroyed unless the wreckage was found in the area and that 'they could not find wreckage of aircraft shot at in the dark because they came down in the sea'. Mr Williamson seemed to think that this happened quite frequently. He concluded by paying tribute to the efficiency of the anti-aircraft gunners.

Reading the reports of the speech one can only say that the officer in question seems to have been rather recalcitrant about attitudes towards the men and women under his command and very cold-hearted, even uncaring, about a raid which had left 125 dead and serious damage in the city.

In September a recruitment drive was begun for the ATC and a substantial part of this was an air exhibition which was housed at the Music Hall. Displays of several hundred model aircraft (including many American and enemy aircraft were included alongside almost every type in service in the RAF) and photographs taken from RAF aircraft were displayed in the round room. The photographs included one of the breach made in the Mohne Dam following the Dambusters raid and others showing RAF aircraft in flight and damage wrought by Bomber Command to German cities. A large number of boys were present and the majority took the opportunity to view the free cinema screening that had been set up showing, on the first day, the ATC's own film *Venture Adventure* and a feature entitled *Towards the Offensive*; other flying-connected films were shown on other days.

The War Comforts Fund went from strength to strength and the end of September saw a celebratory concert held at the Music Hall with the guest of honour being Commander the Marquess of Graham, RNVR. The marquess expressed his thanks on behalf of all the seagoing services for what had been done for them by the 28,000 volunteer knitters and those who worked in the distribution of comforts. By this time there were over 500 branches of the fund in the north-east of Scotland and comforts to the value of £56,000 had been donated thus far. The north-east also had the honour of being the official provider for the reformed 51st Division. A very Scottish-themed show was produced, arranged by the well-known singer Kenneth MacRae, featuring songs in Gaelic and English, Highland dancing, bagpipe music and a dance band.

We have already seen how the Home Guard were increasingly becoming responsible for some of the duties of providing manpower for the manning of anti-aircraft batteries in and around the city. This theme continued throughout the year with increasing numbers of Home Guard units being trained and posted to anti-aircraft batteries. By October the Home Guard had taken over the manning of eight 3.7" anti-aircraft guns at two locations in the city.

In December it was announced that a Torry airman, Flight Sergeant J.F. Clark GM, had taken part in a recently reported raid by three long-range Liberators on a U-boat pack in the Atlantic. Flight Sergeant Clark was a wireless operator/air gunner aboard one of the Liberators. The bombers had successfully sunk five U-boats and damaged three more. The attack was pressed home with great determination as the pack was closing on a convoy and one of the Liberators lost its trailing aerial which caught on the conning tower of a submarine. Flight Sergeant Clark had already survived one nasty incident in training during 1941. On 26 July of that year he had been at 21 OTU and had taken part in a night navigational flight which had resulted in his Wellington aircraft (N2753) losing power and crash landing in Buckinghamshire. One of the crew was injured but Clark had emerged uninjured from the wreckage.

CHAPTER 6

1944 – A Momentous Year

With the Home Guard now even more active in the defence of Britain through the manning of anti-aircraft batteries, there was a question of how to provide sufficient manpower for these added duties. The solution was for a system of link battalions which provided initial training before the men were assessed for suitability for service in an anti-aircraft unit. This system did work but there were still some problems of securing men of sufficient ability for the new work. In April the Aberdeen Z-rocket Battery and Heavy Anti-Aircraft Battery found that of the 94 men provided by its link battalion, the 4th Aberdeenshire, only 27 had proven themselves to be of an adequate quality for the work. This was, according to Colonel Bowhill of the 20th Home Guard Anti-Aircraft Regiment, despite a policy in which commanding officers of batteries had been instructed to show some lenience in their assessments in the hope that many men would improve with time. Lessons were learned and it was agreed to look into the possibility of bringing the 7th Aberdeenshire (Works) Battalion into the scheme as an additional link battalion.

The link system, however, could bear fruit and just a month after Colonel Bowhill's damning assessment, the commanding officer of 71st (Aberdeen) Heavy Anti-Aircraft Battery wrote to express his delight to the commanding officer of 4th Aberdeen Battalion. He stated that a recent intake had been so impressively trained that they had quickly learned the required skills for artillery work, had become skilled gunners in record time and were the equal of any other gunner in his battery.

For those serving in the Home Guard in 1944 (and not all were now volunteers) this was a period of some peculiarity. There was undoubtedly some weariness amongst the Home Guard now as many saw the threat of invasion as being non-existent. On the other hand, the Home Guard was placed on alert as it was anticipated that the enemy might attempt to use raids using landing or airborne forces to disrupt the country in the lead up to or in the wake of the Allied invasion of Western Europe. To this end the Home Guard went through a further period of re-equipping with more modern weaponry becoming available as regular units themselves re-equipped. The organisation also continued to be remodelled and reorganised. In Aberdeenshire the 4th (City of Aberdeen) Battalion established a new support company into which it placed its anti-tank guns, sub-artillery units and machine-gun platoons, while the neighbouring 5th Battalion (based in and around Turriff) formed a mobile company which was to be responsible for mounting operations across the country, even outside its own usual area of operations.[1]

The issue of new ration books in Aberdeen resulted in some confusion on 23 May with large queues forming at Aberdeen Music Hall. People had been told, by area and street, on which day they should attend to collect their new ration books. The authorities also encouraged a 'good neighbour' policy whereby people could collect ration books for neighbouring families, but also explained that people should be sensible about this and not collect too many books as this might cause delays. On the day when the problems ensued the Food Executive Officer, Mr A. Drysdale, explained that the problems had largely been caused by people attending on the incorrect day, while further delays had been caused by people who had not signed their identity cards or had failed to complete the reference page of their old ration book(s).

The local press continued to provide the Aberdeenshire public with information concerning those who were fighting. On 23 May the *Press and Journal* highlighted the award of the DFC to Pilot Officer Iain Farquhar Gray of 101 Squadron, Bomber Command. Described as having demonstrated consistent devotion to duty, fortitude and skill, the account stated that Pilot Officer Gray's mother lived at 31 Salisbury Terrace, Aberdeen, while his late father had been a prominent solicitor in Buckie. Pilot officer Gray (27) had been educated at Aberdeen University where he was a medical student. He interrupted his fourth year of studies in 1942 to join the RAF and volunteer for aircrew duties.

Girl Repatriated After Five Years in Germany

We have already heard how Irene Cooper (then aged 12) had been stranded in the Rhineland in September 1939. Irene had spent the last five years in Germany, staying with a friend of her family and working in a butcher's shop as well as attending

Ms Irene Cooper taken when in Germany. (Press & Journal)

school, but in late May her father, Mr John Cooper, received notification that his daughter, now 17, was at Barcelona awaiting passage aboard the MS *Gripsholm* and a return home.[2]

Irene's return did raise some questions, however. Writing in the *Daily Record* a German exile in Britain expressed his professional and personal concerns. Dr Edgar Stern-Rubarth had worked in the German Foreign Office in pre-Nazi Germany and pointed out that having witnessed what Nazi education had done to schoolchildren in Germany it was possible that Irene may have been influenced by this ideology while she attended the equivalent of secondary school in the town of Eschweller. Dr Stern-Rubarth did, however, provide some encouragement by stating that the area of Eschweller was an area which was not as fanatically pro-Nazi as many other areas of Germany. He stated that Miss Cooper may have been able to be protected from abuse by Nazi officials and ordinary Germans if the family with which she was staying had been in favour with the local Nazi representatives. The doctor also expressed an interest in whether Miss Cooper had been ordered or allowed to join the Association of German Girls and worked in agricultural or forestry camps as a result.

As the MS *Gripsholm* sailed from Barcelona bound for Belfast, Irene Cooper did not know but she was not far away from her brother, John who was a member of the Royal Artillery and was fighting in the Anzio beachhead.[3]

The *Gripsholm* was carrying 638 sick and/or wounded military repatriates on this journey along with 22 civilians, the majority of them women. Irene and the other civilians aided the crew in caring for the service personnel until they arrived at Belfast from where those bound for Britain were transferred to a ship for Liverpool. Arriving after the blackout on the night of 28 May, Irene was met by her father and an aunt, Mrs Frost, who had travelled down from Aberdeen and Leicester respectively. The 17-year-old was barely recognisable to them, described as a chubby 12-year old with plaits when they last saw her in 1939, Irene was now a petite young woman. The family were overcome with Irene, described in the press as the 'Heroine of the Repatriates', immediately collapsing into her father's arms. The family group sought refuge from the pressing crowd behind a police box and hugged for several minutes. Irene commented that she simply wanted her family and no-one else before determinedly adding 'I have looked after myself for five years and I don't want anyone to look after me now.'[4]

At least six other Aberdonians were aboard the MS *Gripsholm*, all were servicemen, with three being from the RAMC. The first was Colonel David P. Levack, RAMC, a well-known Aberdeen radiologist. The second officer was Captain William M. Davidson, RAMC who had been a lecturer in morbid anatomy at Aberdeen University before the war and was the son of a former mathematics master at Aberdeen Grammar School. His wife and son were living at Ardenlea, Ballater. The remaining RAMC servicemen were Private Richard G. Milne, of 12 Millbank Lane and Private Douglas A. Barron of 2 Crimon Place, Aberdeen. Private Barron was the eldest son of his family and had been captured in 1940 when the 51st Division surrendered at St Valery before spending the next four years in a PoW camp in Poland. The remaining Aberdonian servicemen were Private Douglas Dunbar who had been taken prisoner in June 1940 and Private Alexander Brockie, Gordon Highlanders. Private Dunbar worked for the LMS at Drumlithie before the war and his parents lived at Glenbervie Road, Aberdeen. Private Brockie had also been taken prisoner at St Valery and had lived with his wife and three children at Craigton Cottage, Cults, Aberdeen. Private Brockie was another eldest son with his parents living at Northcote Cottage, Pitfodels, Aberdeen.

Captain W M Davidson. (Press & Journal)

The Cooper family took an immediate train bound for Aberdeen arriving there on the afternoon of 29 May. Arriving at Aberdeen Joint Station, there was no publicity and the family negotiated their way through the crowds without being recognised before queuing outside for a taxi to take them to the home of Irene's sister, Mrs Lawson, at 20 Canal Street where a family reunion awaited them. While waiting in the queue Mr Cooper reassured his daughter that she would soon be home.

Upon arriving at Canal Street, Mr Cooper shouted out 'Here's Irene' at which her sister, Mrs Lawson, ran from her house to the sister whose arrival she had been awaiting. The two women embraced tearfully while relatives and friends who had been invited gathered around awaiting their turn to welcome Irene back. All remarked on how pleased they were to see her looking so fit and cheerful with her younger sister, Ella (who had been only 10 when Irene left for Germany), commenting on how much she had grown.

One of the first things that Irene did was to change into the kilt which she had taken with her to Germany. She revealed that she had worn it frequently while in Germany, after letting down the hem as she grew, along with a tartan tam-o'-shanter complete with feathered cockade. After all, she stated, 'I am a Scot and proud of it.' Irene also revealed that the Germans amongst whom she had lived had never seen a kilt before and that, as a result, they called her 'Scottie'.[5] Mrs Lawson commented that Irene seemed to have brought back more clothes with her than she had taken.

Talking about her experiences Irene wistfully examined the familiar family photographs on the wall. She explained that she had been given the opportunity to learn German which was vital if she were to attend school, but that she was given no opportunity to continue her studies of English and as a result she spoke with a slight German accent. Several friends and family members joked with her about this, but her father interrupted by inviting her to recite a few Scots verses. She did, and afterwards

Above left: *Irene and her Father at Aberdeen Joint Station.* (Press & Journal)

Above right: *Irene and her Sister Embrace.* (Press & Journal)

thanked her 'Da'.[6] Irene was questioned about the food situation in Germany to which she replied that she had always had plenty (in contrast with other repatriates who talked of poor and inadequate food) and revealed that she had been permitted to bring back a number of presents for family members.

While there were other family members yet to be visited, Irene was tired from her experiences and her long journey and said that she intended to have a good rest, probably going into the countryside to recuperate, before undertaking these visits. She also revealed that during her voyage she had formed friendships with several of the Aberdeen repatriates including Colonel Levack and Captain Davidson.

Aberdonians were scattered far and wide during the war with many men and women serving in various foreign theatres of action. In late May the Aberdeen press heralded the return of one such Aberdonian. Miss M.C. Laing was a nurse who had served in France as a sister in the Territorial Army Nursing Service (TANS) during the First World War. After the end of that conflict she returned to take charge at Kepplestone Nursing Home in Aberdeen. During the inter-war period she remained on the reserve list of the TANS and was promoted to matron. Upon being called up at the start of the war Miss Laing oversaw the organisation of a Scottish General Hospital which was dispatched, under her charge, to the Middle East in June 1940. The hospital went on to become one of the largest in the Middle East theatre and could cater for 2,400 patients. Miss Laing was also given charge of a nearby PoW hospital with a further 600 beds. She was responsible for overseeing eighty nurses along with other nursing and orderly staff and had to put up with nightly encroachments from local wildlife including jackals, scorpions and rats.

Miss Laing related one of her many experiences to the local press. When the hospital was being cleared prior to being brought back to Britain there was only one Scottish soldier left behind, a Glasgow man too badly injured to be moved. Along with his comrades he had sunk into depression which was deepened when he heard that there was to be an influx of Italian PoW patients. He asked Miss Laing for a separate room, expressing his hatred of 'Eyties', saying he would never speak a civil word to any of them and he would kill any that came near him. The Glaswegian got his small private room but one afternoon there was a football match taking place outside and, knowing that he was a keen football fan, the matron arranged to have him moved outside so he could watch. Shortly afterwards Miss Laing observed the man sitting talking about the match to a blind Italian soldier. Later that night Miss Laing went to check on the Glaswegian soldier and found him in bed with the blind Italian sitting beside him, both men listening to the radio. She said he had looked at her almost apologetically and explained saying 'You see, matron … this poor Eytie canna see, an' he's awful fond of music'.[7]

The Salute the Soldier Campaign

With the Salute the Soldier campaign due to take place during the final week of May and first days of June, the people and organisations of Aberdeen were making their preparations. In order to aid the campaign, the Aberdeen Savings Bank operated extended opening hours in all of its Aberdeen branches. From Saturday 28 May to Wednesday 31 May (excluding Sunday) they were open from 9.30am to 4.30pm; Thursday 1 June saw the branches open during the same hours plus from 6-8pm; on Friday 2 June they were open from 9.30am until 6pm and on Saturday 3 June from 9.30am to 4.30pm.

The days preceding the launch of the campaign saw a concerted drive in the newspapers to persuade the public to support it. On 26 May the *Press & Journal* ran a story itemising the costs of various items of infantry equipment. Describing a bayonet charge in the desert by a unit of Highlanders, the story related how the advance was held up by the presence of an enemy 88mm gun. The infantry immediately sent back reports of the gun and over radio gave the location and co-ordinates allowing their own artillery to destroy the gun and allow them to continue their advance. The portable wireless sets which had saved the day, the article explained, cost £20 and many more would be needed for the forthcoming assault on Europe. Did the money to buy one of these sets, the article queried, lie forgotten in an Aberdeen stocking. If so then the money must be used next week to further the Salute the Soldier campaign. With the campaign setting out to raise £3,000,000 for the Highland Division the article included an extract which explained how the Highlanders and modern warfare in general depended upon accuracy and weight of artillery fire. Because of this there was a great need for an ever-larger number of 25-pounder guns. Each gun cost £2,250 and maintaining an entire regiment of the guns cost £750,000. The list of items went on with a Valentine tank being priced at £10,000, a Bren Carrier at £1,000, a grenade at 2s 6d and a Sten gun bullet at 1d.

For the family of William Watson Robertson, Royal Corps of Signals, of 3 Rosebank Place, Aberdeen, the events in Italy and Salute the Soldier campaign must have seemed particularly poignant as they had just received news that the signaller was lying in a hospital in the central Mediterranean seriously wounded by a shell. Thankfully, it seems that Robertson recovered from his injuries and returned home.

The Salute the Soldier campaign came at a fortuitous time as many an Aberdonian was keenly focussed on events in the Italian Campaign. News of the successful breakout of Allied forces from the Anzio beachhead had just been announced in the days before the campaign began and shortly before this the news of the breaking of the Gustav Line and the collapse of the Senger Line, following the immensely costly Battle of Monte Cassino, had also been announced to a receptive public.[8] An article in the *Press & Journal* of 29 May stated that the victories were indeed important, but cautioned the Aberdonian public that the German forces in Italy were by no means on the run and that important and probably costly battles still lay ahead in that theatre with Rome yet to fall and the forces of Kesselring preparing further defensive lines. The writer went on to say that perhaps the greatest value of the victories in Italy were that they came on the eve of the widely-anticipated invasion of Western Europe and that the victories in Italy had shown that the Allied soldiers were every bit the equal of the Nazi forces and could win conclusive victories just as they had done against the Italians.

Quoting Field Marshal Lord Milne, the article went on to explain how the Aberdeen target of £3,000,000 would normally supply the reformed 51st Division for four months in a sustained campaign such as that fought in Italy and in the anticipated Western Europe invasion this sum would probably be expended by artillery assets within a single month. In conclusion, the article bluntly told Aberdonians that if the Army, Royal Navy and RAF lacked munitions, equipment and food then the war would be needlessly prolonged with greater casualties and serious impact upon Britain. Therefore, it was the duty of every Aberdonian to throw his or her every effort behind the Salute the Soldier campaign and to give every spare penny. Alongside the article was the second part of a piece from a book entitled *The Gordons in North Africa and Sicily*. This further highlighted the efforts of the local regiment and the importance of the Army at this time.

The main focal point for the campaign was provided by the display of a giant picture of a soldier in battledress, with rifle at the ready, which was erected in front of the Music Hall on Union Street. The soldier stood over 24' tall and his boots alone measured over 4' in length. The picture was flanked on both sides by displays of patriotic slogans and posters, while the figure raised by the people of the city was displayed below the soldier and updated daily. The Town House was also decorated for the campaign and a daily adjusted tally was also on display here. Local shops got in on the act and over forty window displays were organised encouraging the people of the city to ensure that the target of £3,000,000 was successfully achieved (this represents over £115 million today).

A great many sporting events had been organised including several which sought to involve the local children in the campaign. These included an exhibition of paintings and drawings by the schoolchildren of the city at the Art Gallery, Schoolhill. This exhibition was opened on the first day of the campaign by the Right Honourable Lord Alness.

Amongst the other events which were scheduled to begin on the first day was a military display at Hazlehead. This included a display by the Royal Artillery, a mobile Bofors anti-aircraft gun, an exhibition of field cooking and other military fieldcrafts and performances by a band of the Gordon Highlanders. The display ground opened at 7pm and the display was open for two hours on the first night. On the following two days the exhibition continued but a band of the Seaforth Highlanders replaced the Gordons and the opening hours were 3-4pm and 7-8pm. Admission to the display ground was 1s for adults and 6d for children under the age of 14, the money raised being donated to the campaign.

A formal inauguration dinner for the campaign was held at the Douglas Hotel on Saturday 27 May. The Lord Provost was joined at the luncheon by Field Marshal Lord Milne, Lord Alness, local MPs and ranking commanders from all the forces along with numerous city and county dignitaries. During his speech to the assemblage Lord Milne urged Aberdeen to try to double the target of £3,000,000 and to view that target figure as a bare minimum to support the 51st Division. He spoke of his immense pride in the young men of Aberdeen who had already gone to fight and the large numbers who had already lost their lives in the nation's cause.

He urged the parents of these men to be proud but told the assembly that the only way in which they could repay such men was through their 'generosity in giving in the same spirit as they gave'. In a rather blatant attempt to rally local pride he went on to tell the assembly that the 'reputation of our city depends on this week. If you don't maintain it the army will be poorer not only by a sum of money but also by your soul. Are you to be worthy of them?' Lord Milne then went on to highlight how in the near future thousands of young British men would be thrown across the Channel in what he described as 'the greatest military adventure that had ever happened in the history of the world'. Describing the thought of the coming campaign as awe-inspiring he went on to say that the future of humanity depended on the success of the venture.

Towards the conclusion of his speech Lord Milne urged small savers to do more for the campaign than had hitherto been the case, telling them that they must not fall into the trap of complacency, as after the Nazis had been defeated the war against Japan still had to fought to a successful conclusion.

Thanking Lord Milne for his words, Lord Alness also added his own urging the population to do its utmost to back the Salute the Soldier campaign. He, however, also referred to Aberdeen's already fine record in supporting the war savings campaigns, pointing out that the city had already saved the total sum of £23,366,000 during the course of the war (over £901 million today).

Lord Milne then departed to take part in several events, including handing out prizes for the schoolchildren's slogan competition at the City Cinema, while Lord Alness performed a similar duty for the art competition at the Art Gallery before he addressed Broadford workers and handed out certificates which had been won in the firm's savings scheme.

The undoubted highlight of the first day of the campaign was a large military parade which assembled in the West End and marched down to Union Street, passing by and saluting Lord Milne at the Music Hall, accompanied by music from no less than seven military bands. Those amongst the thronging crowds who assembled near to the ends of the route could hear the skirl of pipes intermingled with the harsher notes of military bands. At the saluting stand the music was provided by the Seaforth Highlanders who played a selection of music according to the units which passed. *Hearts of Oak* greeted the Naval contingent which led the parade, while Army units were greeted with renditions of *Heilan Laddie* and *The Cock o' the North* amongst others.

The marching column was so large that it took three-quarters of an hour for the parade to pass by the saluting base and the huge crowds were treated to sights such as the men of a mountain artillery unit leading their mules, while a detachment of the ATS from a local anti-aircraft battery drew remarks on their smart appearance as they marched past in battledress and gaiters. Other highlights were a large turn-out from the Home Guard with a white-haired First World War colonel marching as a sergeant in his local Home Guard platoon and a cadet unit which marched past with the precision and pride of a unit of the Guards.

Above: *ATS from an AA Unit
Parade through Aberdeen.*
(Press & Journal)

Right: *The Military Parade.*
(Press & Journal)

Units (in marching order) taking part in Aberdeen Salute the Soldier parade

Seaforth Highlanders Band
Royal Navy
WRNS
Sea Cadets
ITC Pipe Band
Mountain Artillery
Coastal Defence Gunners
Anti-Aircraft Gunners
Infantry (various regimental contingents)
ATS
ITC Military Band
Home Guard Anti-Aircraft Units
4th Battalion Home Guard Pipe Band
4th Battalion Home Guard
6th Battalion Home Guard
7th Battalion Home Guard (and Pipe Band)
STC Pipe Band
STC Battalion Home Guard
Army Cadet Force
ATC Band
RAF
WAAF
ATC
Rangers
GTC
Girls' Guildry

The military display and exhibition at Hazlehead also proved a great draw with a once-per-minute tram service being necessary at times to transport the crowds. Once at Hazlehead the undoubted highlight was the display provided by the men of the mountain artillery unit. They first treated the crowds to a drill display, but the true thrill of the display was towards the end when the men returned in full battledress and demonstrated the speed with which they could go into action. The unit, with its mules, galloped into the arena before assembling their guns in a very speedy fashion to the delight of the crowd. This was followed by a demonstration 'mule ride' in which battery drivers rode their mules over a series of low hurdles and other obstacles in a

Officers of a Mountain Artillery unit give a display of hurdling. (Press & Journal)

display which thrilled the assembled crowds. A group of officers also gave a display of horsemanship as they charged over a hurdle course much to the appreciation of the audience.

Away from these more active demonstrations there was still plenty to interest the public with many of the displays giving civilians a glimpse into Army life during wartime. One showed off a variety of field cookers and the range of food they could provide the soldier in the field; another neighbouring marquee housed a field bakery which also provided snacks for the crowd. Still others showed off mobile workshops and stores which enabled the Army to maintain itself in the field given the increasingly mobile and mechanised nature of warfare.

While Lord Milne could be understood in his urging of small savers, this category had in fact already made a notable contribution on the first day of the campaign with savings bank depositors contributing over £20,000 (over £771,000 today).

The ATS also put on a display at their headquarters during which they held an exhibition of handicrafts. Entries for the competition came from girls who were serving throughout the North Highland Area. The entries included beautiful examples of sewing, embroidery, knitted garments and toys, examples of decorative handiwork and ideas for making do. Large crowds visited the exhibition including the Lord Provost, Sir Thomas Mitchell, and General and Mrs Hamilton of Skene. Tea was served to the auspicious visitors along with a series of dainties and cakes which had been saved from rations by the ATS. Chief Commander Finlay, the head of the ATS in the North Highland Area, announced the winners and distributed the prizes to the following entrants: Junior Commander MacDonald, Corporal E.M. Storer, Sergeant M.R. Emslie, Private B. MacDonald, Corporal H.C.M. Christie, Private M. Grant, Private N. Harper, Lance Corporal L.F. Hannah (winner of two prizes), Private M.R. Coull and Staff Sergeant C. Fyvie.

Breakdown of Contributions on First Day of the Salute the Soldier Campaign

Savings Category	£	S	D
2½% National Savings Bonds	265,200		
3% Savings Bonds	27,455		
3% Defence Bonds	9,835		
National Savings Certificates	7,865	15	
Savings Bank Deposits	20,960		
Savings Stamps	1,585	8	6
Gift Tokens	22	10	
Free Gifts	1		

Although Sunday remained traditionally sacrosanct, the campaign continued in its efforts to raise funds for the Salute the Soldier campaign with the military exhibition continuing to attract large crowds. The second day of the campaign culminated in a Garrison Theatre entertainment at a very crowded Music Hall. The show incorporated a variety of entertainments and ended with a cavalcade of flags from the Allied nations, followed by the national anthems and a silence for the fallen before a striking tableau of Peace surrounded by the uniformed service personnel of the Allies took the stage. Sheriff Laing then introduced Lord Milne to the crowd and he gave a short speech during which he thanked the band of the Gordon Highlanders for providing music for the night (he shook hands with Bandmaster Williams) before praising those members of the audience who were in uniform and wishing them good fortune in the tests that lay ahead. Lord Milne completed his speech by making a further appeal for the people of Aberdeen to get fully behind the week-long campaign and to raise as much money as possible.

The second day of campaigning was even more successful with over double the amount from the first day raised. Almost £950,000 was raised on this second day and by the end of the day the total figure raised was £1,374,961. Small investors once again played a substantial role in the raising of funds with over £846,000 raised through National War Bonds.

Breakdown of Contributions on the Second Day of the Salute the Soldier Campaign

Savings Category	£	S	D
2½% National Savings Bonds	846,600		
3% Savings Bonds	47,900		
3% Defence Bonds	9,820		
National Savings Certificates	11,644		

Savings Bank Deposits	23,149	4	7
Savings Stamps	2,913	15	
Gift Tokens	3	10	
Free Gifts	6		

With the popularity of the campaign and with companies keen to demonstrate their patriotism and willingness to get behind the war effort, several companies made large donations of over £5,000 on the second day of the campaign.

Large Donations on the Second Day of the Salute the Soldier campaign

Company	Amount
Aberdeen & Northern Friendly Society	£8,000
Atlas Assurance Co.	£5,000
Commercial Union Assurance Co.	£5,000
Co-operative Permanent Building Society	£5,000
Halifax Building Society	£20,000
London & Lancashire Insurance Co.	£5,000
North British & Mercantile Insurance Co.	£10,000
Pearl Assurance Co.	£10,000
Sun Life Assurance Society	£5,000
Marks & Spencer Ltd	£5,000
F.W. Woolworth & Co.	£5,000
Legal & General Assurance Society	£5,000
Royal Insurance Co.	£5,000

Staff at the Savings Committee headquarters on Union Street reported a fairly busy day as a steady stream of small investors called at the central selling depot. Once again, the military displays at Hazlehead drew large crowds while other events both large and small ensured that the campaign continued to steadily increase the total raised.

By 1 June the total amount raised stood at £2,681,791 and the committee, impressed by how the people of the city had reacted in this the sixth year of war, took the decision to raise the target for the campaign to £3,500,000. On the final day of May some £765,490 had been contributed and enthusiasm remained undimmed. Amongst the donations was one of £20,000 by Aberdeen Journals Ltd.

The first two days had seen the crowds thrilled by the demonstrations given by the horse and mule men of a mountain artillery battery and on the final day of May it was the turn of an RASC Pack Transport Company to demonstrate their skills. A record crowd was present at Hazlehead to witness the show, which had been specially created for the Salute the Soldier campaign. The display was very well choreographed and included a dozen Highland ponies from Lord Lovat's estate as well as a show of mounted wrestling where the riders attempted to force each other off their horses through hand-to-hand combat. This drew gasps from the audience as it was clear that if any man were brought off his horse there was a danger of him being trampled. This was followed by a display of vaulting and trick-riding by riders mounted upon white horses and then by a pack demonstration in which each horse carried two 112lb packs. There were also displays of tent-pegging, jumping and trick-riding, while the riders performed a variety of actions including reading a book, lighting a cigarette, drinking from a bottle and combing their hair while they took their horses over hurdles and other obstacles. There was a circus-like nature about many of the events which included one soldier who was clad in a ballet dress standing on two ponies while the men riding the Highland ponies appeared dressed as clowns. On 1 June the men of the unit paraded through Aberdeen drawing a substantial crowd.

With the Salute the Soldier campaign proving so popular, the target figure of £3,000,000 was twice revised with a final target of £4,000,000 being set. The final tally was announced on Saturday 3 June and it was revealed that £4,024,862 had been raised.

With the massive invasion underway the squadrons of the RAF were tasked with giving every possible support to the ground forces and to protecting the convoys crossing the Channel. Amongst the more unusual activities was that of 69 Squadron. Based at RAF Northolt as part of the 2nd Tactical Air Force (TAF) and equipped with the obsolescent Vickers Wellington XIII, the squadron was tasked with reconnaissance flights at night, dropping flares to identify German troop movements. The squadron had only just completed training for this role and its first operations were on the night of D-Day. However, it was while on a training exercise in the early hours of D-Day that Aberdeen-born Squadron Leader Alexander George Dawson (32) lost his life. Squadron Leader Dawson and his crew were on a night exercise when the starboard engine of their Wellington XIII (JA619) lost power and Squadron Leader Dawson decided to make an emergency landing at RAF Wratting Common just after 1am. Tragically, a Stirling of 1615 Heavy Conversion Unit (HCU), based at Wratting Common, had earlier burst a tyre on landing and was on the runway awaiting removal and the Wellington of Squadron Leader Dawson ploughed into the Stirling before bursting into flames which quickly engulfed the two bombers. It took the combined efforts of Wratting Common's fire appliance and those of the NFS from nearby Haverhill and Balsham to bring the fire under control and it was not until two hours later that the bodies of Squadron Leader Dawson and one of his crew, Flight Sergeant C.J. Gubbins, were recovered. Of the five-man crew two were killed and two injured.

An essential part of the D-Day invasion was the capture of bridges and crucial towns by American and British airborne troops. A massive force of aircraft was needed to drop paratroopers and to tow gliders across the Channel and into the teeth of the enemy defences. Amongst the RAF squadrons taking part was 620 Squadron based at RAF Fairford. It had initially been a heavy bomber squadron before switching roles to making covert drops to support the Special Operations Executive (SOE) but it was required to drop elements of the 5th Parachute Brigade. Between them the aircraft of 620 and 190 Squadrons carried 887 paratroopers to Drop Zone-N (DZ-N), near Ranville. Twenty-three of 620 Squadron's Stirlings took off on the night of 5 June; three were shot down carrying out their operations while it was discovered upon return that many of the aircraft had suffered damage. Amongst those lost was the Stirling of Aberdonian navigator Flight Sergeant Henry Mark Bittiner (22) who is buried in a communal grave at Ranville War Cemetery.

Amongst the paratroopers were several units of parachute-trained squadrons of the Royal Engineers. They were tasked with a variety of objectives including the de-mining of bridges and the destruction of defences. One of these units was 591 (Antrim) Squadron, ordered to destroy anti-aircraft obstacles and defences. In the event the unit was badly scattered. One Stirling containing men of the unit was shot down and crash-landed at Chateau-de-Grangues. The disorientated survivors were quickly captured by German troops and taken to the chateau. In a second wave were troops from the squadron aboard Horsa gliders. Four of these were also driven off-track and crash-landed at the chateau. Once again, the troops were quickly captured and taken to the chateau stables. Shortly afterwards those who were seriously injured were driven to a nearby hospital leaving eight men tied up in the stables. Amongst them was 22-year old Aberdonian Driver George Thomson. His parents received the news that their son had been reported missing in July followed by a further telegram the next month informing that he was now believed to have been killed. The truth was far more disturbing and not fully established until shortly after the war.

The eight men, including Driver Thomson, had been led from the stables shortly after 2am and made to lie face down outside. The officer in charge of the chateau, Stabsfeldwebel Herman Vieseler, then murdered the men by shooting each once in the lower back and then in the back of the neck. The murders were witnessed by a Frenchman and the Comte of the chateau asked the German why he had done such a vile deed and was told a variety of unfeasible stories. The truth was that he had done so to impress some of his hard-line superiors and, indeed, he was subsequently awarded the Iron Cross. The bodies were initially just thrown into ditches but the nanny at the chateau was an older Irish woman and she took a cart, recovered the bodies, and took them for a more respectful burial (they were later moved to Ranville War Cemetery).[9]

At least one more Aberdonian lost his life on D-Day. Signalman Douglas Milne of 6th Airborne Division Signals (Royal Corps of Signals) was killed and is buried at the Bayeaux War Cemetery. Milne was 22 at the time of his death, his parents, James and Bella, lived at Rosemount. He was a married man, leaving a widow, Rose, in West Hartlepool, County Durham.

With bomb damage to many properties and the lack of building a hallmark of the war, there was a serious shortage of available housing in Aberdeen and, as thoughts turned to a future peace, the Town Council assessed that 2,500 extra houses were required in the city. The Housing Committee was well aware of the problem as only sixteen houses had been constructed during July bringing the total for the year to just 56. A meeting of the Housing Committee on 28 August agreed to make an application to the government for 2,500 factory-built houses to be allocated for the city. Councillor G.R. McIntosh told the local press that he was unsure of whether the houses would be of the 'Portal' type, a timber model of which had been displayed at the Old Infirmary Buildings the previous month.[10] There were a number of different types of prefabricated housing types available from several companies, all of which had been designed according to a government specification and Councillor McIntosh also informed the press that it was hoped that once the government had approved the design a Tarran-designed house was to be displayed in the city.[11]

The Home Guard was stood down on 3 December and many Aberdonian men were left adrift without the purpose that the Home Guard had given them. The force had become a far more effective and efficient organisation than it had presented during its early, ramshackle, existence. The weaponry had increased beyond recognition as shown in the 2nd Aberdeenshire Battalion's inventory of personal weapons. The list below does not include weapons such as pistols, hand grenades and the Northover Projector (a device which launched grenades over distances of up to 200 yards).[12]

2nd Aberdeenshire Battalion, Home Guard, Weapons Upon Stand-down

Weapon	Number
Browning Automatic Rifle (BAR)	50
Browning medium machine-gun	6
Lewis light machine-gun	18
Rifle (.300)	1,008
Rifle (.303)	28
Rifle (0.55), anti-tank	12
Smith gun	14
Spigot mortar	12
Sten sub-machine gun	602
Vickers medium machine-gun	2
2-pounder anti-tank gun	4

Despite this, the battalion was still surprisingly lacking in some items. The majority (54 per cent) of Home Guardsmen in the battalion were apparently armed with .300 rifles (probably the American Ross rifles) rather than the regular Army standard .303 Lee-Enfield rifle, while the battalion was still severely lacking medium machine-guns and anti-tank weapons. On a more positive note they had an adequate supply of sub-machine guns with 32 per cent of the battalion having access to the temperamental but effective Sten gun.

CHAPTER 7

1945 – A Hard-Earned Victory, and Defeat

As Aberdeen welcomed in the seventh year of the war many held the cherished hope and belief that the conflict, at least in Europe, might at last be entering its final stages. It was clear to most that the Germans were finished but that it might take a little time until they were forced into surrender. The war against Japan, however, was a different story and although the Japanese forces were in retreat on many fronts, they were not giving in easily and there was little sign that their leaders were considering surrender. Many believed that a costly and bitterly fought campaign would be required to finally knock the Japanese out of the war. Many Aberdonians were already fully aware of the brutality that the Japanese were capable of and a number were anxiously awaiting news of loved ones whom they knew to be prisoners of the Japanese.

William and Jane McAllan believed that their son, James, was a prisoner of war of the Japanese but in the final year of the war they received the news that he had died in captivity on 20 January. Like so many who died in Japanese custody as PoWs his body was never recovered, and he is commemorated on the Singapore Memorial.

The authorities in Aberdeen were preparing for the news of German surrender and the possible implications for the expected VE-Day celebrations. Monday 7 May was scheduled as the Aberdeen spring holiday and the council informed people that if VE-Day fell on that day or the two preceding days then the spring holiday would be postponed until 4 June.

As it happened the long-awaited day was 8 May and the people of Aberdeen reacted with relief and happiness. Kirk bells in Aberdeen and in surrounding towns and villages pealed and in most places families gathered around the radio to listen to the Prime Minister. In many of the coastal communities, ships and boats sounded hooters and whistles while several celebrated by firing off maroons. Inland many communities set light to hastily prepared bonfires and public buildings and homes were quickly bedecked with bunting and flags.

A crowd of over 1,000 gathered in front of the Town House, cheering when the flags of the allied nations were flown. As church bells began pealing anew the crowd began waving flags which they had brought along. As the final wailing notes of the last all-clear was sounding Lord Provost Mitchell, who had listened to the broadcast with other members of the council, stepped out onto the balcony to address the crowd. After giving his thanks for the ending of the war in Europe he said that he felt joy that they were now entering 'a period of peace and goodwill'. He then went on to remind the crowd that in many Aberdeen houses the rejoicing was strongly tempered by sadness and grief. In these homes, he went on, 'rejoicing was impossible because

Crowd outside the Town House. (Aberdeen Weekly Journal)

a father, a son, or a brother has been given to pay the supreme sacrifice' and where the day would bring sad memories of loved ones never to return. In concluding his speech, the Lord Provost reminded the people that a great effort would be required to 'build a new and better world'. The crowd immediately applauded and sang 'For he's a jolly good fellow' before bursting into a spontaneous rendering of the National Anthem. Although a few thunder-flashes were set off, most of the crowd dispersed quietly to celebrate in their own way. Shortly after the official announcement a crowd of over 500 gathered to hear a short service at Woodside South Church.[1]

One Aberdeen family amongst those referred to by the Lord Provost heard on the weekend before D-Day that a loved one was now presumed to have lost his life since being missing since 1941. Surgeon Lieutenant Commander Ronald Grant Dingwall OBE had been chief medical officer aboard HMS *Gloucester* when it was sunk by German dive-bombers off Crete. Lieutenant Commander Dingwall (37) was a married man who left a widow and son. A former pupil of Aberdeen Grammar

School, where he was known as a keen sportsman, and a graduate in medicine from Aberdeen University, he was well known in his native Aberdeen.

For many this involved the hasty and urgent gathering of suitable provisions for the planned celebrations. Bread was in particularly short supply and long queues were a feature of the morning and early afternoon as 'housewives besieged the bakeries from the opening hour'. Early risers had bought heavily but the bakeries had been prepared for the rush and had prepared extra batches meaning that, fortunately, there was a sufficient supply. Queues also formed outside butchers' shops at an early hour as people prepared.

A large number of people formed into a parade but, with no organisation, began to aimlessly walk up and down Union Street. Many amongst this crowd were factory workers or shop assistants who had turned up for work as normal only to find that their place of employment was closed for the VE-Day celebrations. Shortly after noon the weather took a hand and heavy rain began to fall. This dampened spirits and cleared the streets. Despite the poor weather large numbers still paraded through the main street cheering and singing.

Lieutenant   Commander R.G. Dingwall of Aberdeen. (Aberdeen Weekly Journal)

In the ballroom of the NAAFI Club in Market Street a large crowd of servicemen and women listened to a short thanksgiving service held by Padre F.G. Findlay, who had been a padre with the British Liberation Army (BLA) in Europe. After this the service personnel listened with rapt attention to the Prime Minister's broadcast before heading out onto the streets to join in the celebrations. At the Gordon Barracks the regimental standard was hoisted as a bugler played the salute before members of the regiment set off smoke canisters in celebration.

Service personnel listed to VE Day broadcast at NAAFI. (Aberdeen Weekly Journal)

Above left: *Regimental standard raised at Gordon Barracks.* (Aberdeen Weekly Journal)

Above right: *Gordon Highlanders set off smoke canisters.* (Press & Journal)

Down the coast at Stonehaven the streets were decorated in good time and, following the broadcast, a large crowd gathered in the Market Square to hear a speech by Baillie Ramsay. During the evening a dance was held at the Town Hall attended by over 500 people. Indeed, so large was the crowd that an overflow dance was held outside in the Market Square. This was the largest number of people ever recorded to have attended a dance in the town. In neighbouring Inverbervie the town officer, Mr D. Duncan, proceeded around the decorated streets for the first time since the war began, ringing his bell to indicate a dance held that evening under the auspices of the Town Council. At Gourdon two church services, held in the afternoon and evening, led by the Rev. W.M. Hendrie, were well attended. Church services were also a feature of VE-Day in Insch where the Rev. J. Hardie Duthie officiated at St. Drostan's Episcopal Church. He also joined in, with Rev. J.E. Penman, the leading of a unified service at Insch Church.

The celebrations at Peterhead were tinged with relief and thanksgiving. Church services were once again well attended. As in most communities, bells pealed and flags were flown and, in Peterhead, Provost Dingwall gave a speech of thanksgiving. Fraserburgh, Buckie and Banff were particularly brightly decorated and, once more, large crowds attended services before celebrating in the streets.

When night fell and the blackout descended, a thick fog had developed over many areas of Aberdeen which dampened the celebrations. Despite the blackout a large bonfire had been lit on Brimmond Hill, but so dense was the fog that even this could be seen from no more than a few yards and many who were going to see the bonfire had to be directed to it.

An Aberdeenshire man proved to be the first man to be decorated at the first investiture held at Buckingham Palace following the end of hostilities. Major Lewis Tevendale of Stonehaven collected the DCM which he had been awarded for his courage while a sergeant major at Ljtani River in Syria during

June 1941. Other Aberdeenshire men were relating their experiences as prisoners of war as they returned to their homeland. One such was Captain David A. Addison of The Moorings, Inverbervie. Captain Addison had been taken prisoner by the German battleship *Gneisenau* and reported that the prisoners had been well treated upon the warship before being dropped off at Brest, from where they were taken to a PoW camp. The first commandant of this camp made the British prisoners stand in the courtyard for hours until all of the men were suffering from frostbite, the second was thought to be too soft and was replaced by the Nazis, but the third showed himself to be a fair man and their treatment improved. The prisoners kept themselves informed of the fighting around them by using illicit wireless sets. Captain Addison related how if a set was found it was placed in a store but that the prisoners were usually able to buy it back from the guards the next day using cigarettes. The camp was liberated by the 51st Division and the Scots Guards.

The official victory celebrations went on for some days and culminated on 13 May in a large victory parade and service of thanksgiving. More than 2,500 men and women of the services and of the civil defence services, along with boys' and girls' associations, took part in the procession which was witnessed by large crowds who lined the route. As the parade assembled in Rubislaw Terrace and Queen's Terrace rain was threatening, but the sun came out as the parade set off led by the 7th Battalion, Home Guard Pipe Band and followed by a naval contingent and Sea Cadets. Seven bands took part in the march to ensure a good pace was kept and a spectacle for the crowds.

Amongst the large Army contingent was a unit of Poles. When reaching the saluting base outside the Music Hall the Poles paraded with their ceremonial, stiff-legged, step which earned a particularly loud cheer from the crowd. Amongst the regular Army units were the men of the Home Guard and the women's and auxiliary services. Following the Army were the RAF, WAAFs and boys from the ATC as well as the men and women of the home services. Led by a contingent from the police, this section consisted of representatives from the NFS, all of the civil defence services, the WVS, the rest centre staff, and the Land Army. Bringing up the rear of the parade were the Red Cross, various youth bodies, the British Legion and the Old Contemptibles' Association. The last two groups were the only ones to carry standards in the parade and these were saluted by the Lord Provost and senior military officers from the saluting base.

The church service which followed the parade saw the West Church of St Nicholas packed by parties from the participating units. The Rev C.P. Millar reminded the congregation that further sacrifice was still needed if the victory was to be the beginning of a better future for all. The official celebrations concluded with a thanksgiving and remembrance service held that night at the Music Hall. Hundreds of people, however, were left disappointed as they could not get in due to the already packed venue. Those who did get in heard a variety of messages, both religious and secular, with music from a choir of 300 drawn from churches across Aberdeen.

Japan Defeated and Peace at Last

By August Japan was on her knees but top Allied strategists were warning politicians that an invasion of Japan itself would possibly lead to huge Allied casualties as fanatical Japanese forces held out to the last. Therefore, American President, Harry S. Truman, authorised the use of the newly developed atomic bombs. The first was dropped on Hiroshima on 6 August and the second on Nagasaki three days later. The appalling damage and casualties convinced the Japanese that further resistance was hopeless. In the days following the bombs being dropped excitement began to build in Aberdeen that the end of the war was in sight.

VJ-Day was 15 August and two days of holidays were allowed for the country to celebrate the end of the Second World War. Just as on VE-Day the people of Aberdeen were in the mood to celebrate but heavy rain persisted throughout the day and this somewhat dampened even the highest spirits. A large crowd, though not as large as three months prior, gathered once more outside the Town House for an official ceremony. Lord Provost Sir Thomas Mitchell, once again, addressed the crowd and once more expressed his sincere sympathies to the many Aberdonian families who had suffered the loss of loved ones during the war and went further, mentioning those who had returned maimed through injury or having suffered cruelty in PoW camps. However, he said that today marked a day of celebration which ended years of barbarism and that it was the duty of everyone to ensure that those who would be returning to the city would find a better future, and jobs, awaiting them. Once again a parade was organised and church services proved very popular.

Service personnel who were regular patrons of the Princess Café found that their bills were marked with a large 'V' and were told that this was the proprietor's way of telling them that their meals on this historic day were on the house.

Large crowds visited the harbour to see the display of flags and bunting which decorated the ships and many more returned at night to see the displays illuminated. The many flags in the city were impressive but not as colourful or plentiful as had marked VE-Day. By nightfall, and despite the weather, large and noisy crowds of mainly young people were packing the streets with singing and fireworks all being constantly heard. For the throngs who had earlier packed into places of entertainment, however, the main aim seemed to be getting home and out of the heavy rain. The Marischal College and the Town House Tower were floodlit and crowds visited these to see the spectacle, so strange after years of blackout, but the rain 'won in the end'.

Once again VJ-Day proved to be 'food queue day for most Aberdeen housewives'. Once again bread was the main problem and, despite bakeries working at top speed, supplies ran out. Butchers' and grocers' shops were also extremely busy as people were determined to stock up in order to be able to celebrate. The butchers agreed to remain open all week but would be closed on Monday and Tuesday the following week, while most grocers opened on VJ-Day itself but were closed on the following day. Tobacco was also in short supply as smokers who wished to buy two days' supply found themselves lucky to obtain enough for just one day and many shops simply ran out and were forced to turn customers away.

The next day saw more celebrations as bonfires blazed in the streets of Aberdeen and crowds of young people celebrated raucously. At Mearns Street, crowds danced around a large bonfire to music supplied by a woman playing the harmonium. Around the quayside and on Castlehill bonfires were lit and attracted crowds of revellers while Torry was also lit by fires. All of the main streets also held firework displays and these too were well attended.

The rain had now abated and thousands of young men and women remained on the streets celebrating until the early hours. Open-air dances at Hazlehead and Duthie Park were big attractions as were the floodlit towers. Further large crowds gathered to watch the Lord Provost light a large bonfire on Brimmond Hill. While fireworks cracked overhead Treasurer Morrison of the Town Council was forced to issue an embarrassing apology for the lack of an official Aberdeen fireworks display. Mr Morrison claimed that the council had placed a large order for fireworks six months previously but that this had not been fulfilled.

Following the end of the war many Aberdeen factories had to rapidly adjust to peacetime conditions with a sudden slackening of orders and a dearth of government contracts as the country immediately began scaling back its armed forces. The Ministry of Aircraft Production (MAP) aero-engine component factory which had been opened in the final year of the war at Tullos was an early victim of

Above left: *Floodlit Marishcal College on VJ Day.* (Press & Journal)

Above right: *Floodlit Town House Tower.* (Press & Journal)

this drawdown. In September the workforce had contracted from a high of 562 in July to just 400. Questions were asked in the House of Commons as to the plans for the factory as it was said to be causing some anxiety and concern in Aberdeen. By 18 October the government was able to confirm that the factory was surplus to MAP's requirements and that the Board of Trade had been asked to explore options for peacetime production at the factory under new ownership.[2]

Despite the talk of a bright new future for Aberdeen and the north-east it was clear that there were going to be many trials ahead for the city and its people. Requirements for extensive rebuilding, the replacement of housing stock, creating and finding jobs for all of the men and women who were returning from service in the forces, all of these tasks faced the city along with uncertainties of a peace-time future following seven years of total warfare.

Endnotes

Chapter 1: 1939 – A Storm Breaks

1. *Aberdeen Weekly Journal*, 7 September 1939, p.1.
2. *Aberdeen Weekly Journal*, 7 September 1939, p.1.
3. HMS *Ebor Wyke* was torpedoed and sunk on 2 May 1945, earning the dubious distinction of being the final British warship to be sunk by a U-boat. The only survivor was her Coxswain, John Milnes.
4. 107 Squadron had sent five Blenheims on the raid and lost four. RAF casualties amounted to 24 per cent of aircraft dispatched to make the attacks.
5. *The Press and Journal*, 24 May 1944, p.4.
6. Although the claim has been questioned it has been officially verified by the RAF. This was not the first German aircraft to be shot down by the British during the war, however. Much to the chagrin of the RAF this honour went to a Blackburn Skua of 803 Squadron Fleet Air Arm (FAA), operating from HMS *Ark Royal*, on 26 September when another Do18 was shot down. The FAA was under the control of the Admiralty and was a branch of the Royal Navy.
7. The SS *St Sunniva* was a passenger vessel which operated on the Aberdeen-Orkney/Shetland route. During the war she served as a guard ship, an accommodation ship and finally a convoy rescue ship. She was believed capsized without warning through icing on or around 21 January 1943 with the loss of all hands. The SS *St Clair* was another passenger vessel, operating on the Leith-Aberdeen-Orkney/Shetland route. She was commandeered by the RN and renamed the HMS *Baldur*, serving as an accommodation ship at Rekjavik before being converted into a convoy rescue ship. She survived the war and was scrapped in 1967.
8. HMS *Courageous* was sunk by a U-Boat with the loss of over 500 of her crew. Able Seaman Borthwick's luck continued and he survived the war.

Chapter 2: 1940 – Into Battle

1. The *Daneden* had led a rather fateful life as she had been declared missing before the war but had returned to port when long overdue.
2. Sergeant Morrice and his crew are commemorated on the Runnymede Memorial.
3. It would appear that George, too, had been taken prisoner.

4. The true scale of the losses on the *Lancastria* have never been fully established. It is known that it is the greatest single vessel loss of life in British maritime history. Since the loss of the *Lancastria* successive British governments have remained curiously reluctant to acknowledge the event, refusing to grant the wreck war-grave status (claiming that this would only be symbolic as it lies in French waters) and repeatedly rejecting the release of documents through the FOIA. In 2015 the government announced that all known documents had been released to the National Archives long ago. See also: https://media.nationalarchives.gov.uk/index.php/forgotten-tragedy-the-loss-of-hmt-lancastria/

5. A Q-ship was a merchant vessel which had been upgraded and heavily armed with concealed weaponry. In the case of the *Willamette Valley* she had started life as the motor merchant *West Lynn* and when converted to a Q-ship she was equipped with Asdic and concealed armament consisting of nine 4" guns, one 12lb gun, four machine guns, four 21" torpedo tubes and 100 depth charges.

6. All of the men killed in the loss of the *River Ness* are commemorated on the Tower Hill Memorial.

7. The attack damaged two trawlers, HMT *Botanic* and HMT *Kingston Chrysoberyl*. HMT *Botanic* was sunk by enemy aircraft on 18 February 1942. Skipper Lees was buried at St. James's Cemetery, Dover.

8. The German crew of four men were all killed, one was found in the escape hatch of the bomber with his parachute harness on, and they were subsequently buried with full military honours at the Old Churchyard at Dyce. The names of the crew were as follows: Leutnant Herbert Huck; Gefreiter Georg Kerkhoff; Unteroffizier Paul Plischke; and Feldwebel August Skokan. Pilot Officer Caister was credited with the victory but was shit down over Calais three months later and spent the rest of the war as a PoW.

9. According to the records of the Commonwealth War Graves Commission.

10. *Aberdeen Weekly Journal*, 18 July 1940, p.1.

11. Happily, unlike in many wartime marriages, the young airman survived the war.

12. Sergeant Cameron has no known grave and is commemorated on the Runnymede Memorial, along with two of his crew. The body of the observer, P/O B.C. Paton was recovered from the sea and buried at Kristiansand.

13. Sgt Cheyne lies in the Asmara War Cemetery, Eritrea.

14. The other crew killed in the accident were Flying Officer A.R. Nivison-Smith (pilot) and Sgt S. Nichols. Flying Officer Nivison-Smith was an Australian serving in the RAF and is buried at Dyce Old Churchyard.

15. *Press & Journal*, 18 November 1940, p.2.

16. *Ibid*.

17. *Aberdeen Weekly Journal*, 5 December 1940, p.3.

18. Sergeant Leslie is buried at Saffron Waldon Cemetery. His pilot was Pilot Officer Frederick George Nightingale (26), RAF, MiD, of Reigate, Surrey.

Chapter 3: 1941 – Defeat after Defeat

1. *Aberdeen Weekly Journal*, 27 March 1941, p.1.
2. Private John (Jack) Hutcheon, 5th Btn, Gordon Highlanders, is buried at Malbork Commonwealth War Cemetery, Poland. He is one of 239 casualties buried there, mainly men who died in captivity.
3. *Aberdeen Weekly Journal*, 27 March 1941, p.1
4. Lord Boyd Orr went on to become Director General of the United Nations Food and Agriculture Organization in 1945 before receiving the Nobel Peace Prize in 1949.
5. *Press & Journal*, 2 June 1941, p.4.

Chapter 4: 1942 – Attrition

1. Osborne, *The People's War*, p.133.
2. *Press & Journal*, 2 March 1943, p.2.
3. *Press & Journal*, 2 March 1942, p.3.
4. *Press & Journal*, 2 March 1942, p.2.
5. *Press & Journal*, 3 March 1942, p.3.
6. *Press & Journal*, 28 March 1942, p.3.
7. Pilot Officer Lewis is buried in his hometown at Springbank Cemetery. Lewis's pilot, P/O Ion Brancovan Constant was a Shirburnian and, while at school, had a reputation for getting into scrapes and his love of adventure.
8. The crew consisted of: F/O Malcolm Graeme Grant (27), RAF (pilot); P/O William Ferries Raffan (25), RAF (2nd pilot); Sgt Ernest Cheetham (21), RAF (navigator/bomb aimer); Sgt Edward Marsden, RAF (navigator/bomb aimer); Flight Sgt James David Maxwell (19), RCAF (wireless operator/air gunner); and Sgt Gilbert Charles James Heywood (20), RAF (air gunner). This was the second loss over the Bay of Biscay in two days for 10 OTU as the crew of F/Sgt Austin had been lost on the previous day.
9. *Press & Journal*, 23 December 1942, p.2.
10. *Press & Journal*, 23 December 1942, p.2.

Chapter 5: 1943 – The Tide Turned

1. The body of the unfortunate Private Greig may have been blown over the cliff and recovered later, or further remains were subsequently found at the site of the incident, as the remains of the young soldier are buried at Christchurch Cemetery.
2. On 10 December 1941 the Japanese had successfully attacked the Shing Mun Redoubt which was held by the Royal Scots, amongst other units, and on the day that Private Gibbs died the Royal Scots were retreating to Hong Kong Island

itself while under sustained attack from the air and from artillery. Private Gibbs is buried at Sai Wan War Cemetery.

3. Osborne, *The People's War*, pp. 159-60.
4. Trooper Hoops is commemorated on the Medjez-El-Bab Memorial in Tunisia.
5. The crew consisted of: Sergeant Alexander Greig (22), RAF (pilot); Flight Sergeant James Mead (24), RAF (2nd pilot); Sgt Douglas William Perch, RAF (flight engineer), Sgt Peter Bailey (21), RAF (navigator), F/Sgt John Campbell Paton (29), RAF (from Glasgow) (bomb aimer), Sgt Charles Victor Ellen (23), RAF (wireless operator), Sgt Norman Frederick Trigg, RAF (air gunner), and WO David Wesley Lowther (28), RCAF (air gunner).
6. *Aberdeen Weekly Journal*, 18 March 1943, p.1.
7. Private Anderson survived his ordeal as a captive.
8. *Press & Journal*, 10 April 1943, p.4.
9. The account was not published, however, until late May.
10. *Aberdeen Weekly Journal*, 20 May 1943, p.1.
11. The claims have continued in some cases even to this day. The Luftwaffe had a particularly poor reputation for accuracy at this point of the war, however, and the difficulties in accurate low-level bombing were experienced by the RAF as well. Indeed, it usually took specially selected aircrew and extensive training to hit such targets with any confidence. The dams raid and several others undertaken by, for example, a number of Mosquito squadrons were very good examples of such raids executed successfully but there were many others which did not succeed.
12. *Press & Journal*, 23 April 1943, p.4.
13. *Press & Journal*, 26 April 1943, p.4.
14. *Ibid*. Little did the people of Aberdeen know it, but this was the last incident of the bombing of a Scottish city during the war.
15. Seaman Gordon has no known grave and is commemorated on the Tower Hill Memorial.
16. *Press & Journal*, 22 April 1943, p.2.
17. *Press & Journal*, 17 July 1943, p.4.
18. Osborne, *The People's War*, pp. 179-80.
19. *Press & Journal*, 4 August 1943, p.4.

Chapter 6: 1944 – A Momentous Year

1. See Osborne, *The People's War*, pp. 205-6.
2. The MS *Gripsholm* was an ocean liner built in 1924 by Armstrong Whitworth at Newcastle for the Swedish-American Line. She was the first ship built for transatlantic express service using a diesel engine rather than steam power. From 1942-1946 the ship was chartered by the US State Dept. to act as an exchange and repatriation ship, operating with a Swedish captain and crew, which carried German and Japanese nationals to neutral ports where they were exchanged for

US and Canadian citizens (along with British citizens who were married to US or Canadians and, as we have seen, selected British citizens). During the four years in which she served in this capacity the *Gripsholm* made twelve round trips and carried almost 28,000 repatriates. After the war the ship was sold and renamed the MS *Berlin*. She worked ferrying immigrants to Canada and she was used as the centre image for the newly designed Canadian passport of 2012. She was sold for scrap in 1966.

3. It would appear that John survived the war.
4. *Press & Journal*, 29 May 1944, p.1.
5. *Press & Journal*, 30 May 1944, p.4.
6. *Ibid*.
7. *Press & Journal*, 26 May 1944, p.4.
8. Although the public knew these victories had been very hard fought, they were largely kept unaware of the true scale of slaughter in the Italian Campaign. The Battle of Monte Cassino had lasted 123 days and resulted in 55,000 Allied casualties, the Battle of Anzio had lasted 136 days and resulted in 43,000 casualties, while the Italian Campaign, which had begun on 10 July 1943 and would last until 2 May 1945, would result in at least 327,000 Allied casualties.
9. A subsequent war crime tribunal held in 1945 discovered credible evidence of war crimes but Veiseler was never found. He is not listed as having been killed or taken prisoner and did not return to his pre-war home.
10. The 'Portal' type houses, named after Housing Minister, Lord Portal, were metal framed bungalows which became known as prefabs.
11. Tarran had prior experience of constructing prefabricated housing and produced three types of house all with an aluminium frame and wall panels made from concrete and chemically-treated sawdust. In the years following the war 19,014 Tarran-type houses were constructed across Britain.
12. Osborne, B.D., *The People's Army. Home Guard in Scotland 1940-1944* (Birlinn, Edinburgh), pp. 94-5.

Chapter 7: 1945 – A Hard-Earned Victory, and Defeat

1. *Aberdeen Weekly Journal*, 10 May 1945, p.1.
2. The Tullos factory was sold and, as Tullos Factory Ltd, began to produce agricultural machinery for both the home and export market but by 1949 a lack of orders had resulted in a third of the workforce being laid off.

Index